Developing
Spiritual Intelligence

Dr Altazar Rossiter is a rare, supportive and friendly presence who is able to facilitate a clear self-look at what may be deeply buried in the heart and hidden from the usual rational consciousness. Highly recommended. **Ravi Ravindra**, Professor of Physics and Comparative Religion at Dalhousie University, Halifax

Altazar invites us to get in touch with our potential; love our light and bless our shadow. Awakening our consciousness, paying attention to our feelings as the source of true learning, he inspires us to give intent to centredness and opening to the wonders of who we are. **Veronica De Andres**, Executive Board of the International Council for Self-Esteem

I expect that every charlatan in history has attempted to pull off what Altazar manages to do...but Altazar is the genuine article. **Lonny Gold**, International Trainer and Lecturer

Altazar Rossiter proves himself to be a master transpersonal psychologist in his book Developing Spiritual Intelligence. *By integrating the spiritual dimension into our complex mental world, Rossiter demonstrates that the mind does not need to be locked into itself and has access to the next level of spirit if we trust its power and co-operate with it through conscious intent. One particular area of interest, not often found in books on the subject, is the power of language and words which can either be detrimental or transformational to our character. Thus the emphasis on affirmations spoken aloud. The defining of terms in the book, so important for clarity, is superb, especially of that illusive word "consciousness." Rossiter presents us with a supreme holistic view of human beings and thus his topics of inquiry include the observer or witness, the wisdom of the heart, the wound of the soul, embodiment and the chakras and psychic abilities.* Developing Spiritual Intelligence *is for any people of sensitivity. Rossiter systemically and intelligibly opens the doors and lets in the divine light, truth and wisdom.* **James D'Angelo**, PhD, author of *The Healing Power of the Human Voice.*

This beautifully clear and fascinating book is an incredibly simple guide to that which so many of us search for: the kind of spiritual intelligence that will enable us to live peacefully, intelligently, and joyfully whatever our circumstances. It brings the spiritual world down to earth, which is just where we need it to be in order to take our next step. **Dr Dina Glouberman** *author of* Life Choices, Life Changes *and co-founder of Skyros*

At last, here is a book that I can give to friends who have not yet engaged with a conscious spiritual path but who are ready to embrace the greater fullness of who they are. In Altazar Rossiter's terms this involves us aligning with "spiritual intelligence". In a way that normalises spirituality as a natural aspect of being human this book gives us ways of drawing on our own innate knowledge and wisdom to access the subtle levels within our contemporary world, focussed as it seems to be on material levels of reality. Other writers are currently urging us to rise above our seeming limitations through an "evolutionary leap". This book offers some practical principles and practices for doing this. **Janice Dolley** Executive Director , Wrekin Trust – University for Spirit Forum, co-author of *The Quest*

Developing
Spiritual Intelligence:
The Power of You

Altazar Rossiter

BOOKS

Winchester, U.K.
New York, U.S.A.

First published by O Books, 2006
An imprint of John Hunt Publishing Ltd., The Bothy,
Deershot Lodge, Park Lane, Ropley, Hants, SO24 0BE, UK
office@johnhunt-publishing.com
www.o-books.net

USA and Canada
NBN
custserv@nbnbooks.com
Tel: 1 800 462 6420
Fax: 1 800 338 4550

Singapore
STP
davidbuckland@tlp.com.sg
Tel: 65 6276
Fax: 65 6276 7119

Australia
Brumby Books
sales@brumbybooks.com
Tel: 61 3 9761 5535
Fax: 61 3 9761 7095

South Africa
Alternative Books
altbook@global.co.za
Tel: 27 011 792 7730
Fax: 27 011 972 7787

Design: Jim Weaver Ltd
Cover design: Book Design, London

ISBN-13: 978 1 905047 64 2
ISBN-10: 1 905047 64 9

A CIP catalogue record for this book is available from the British
Library.

Printed by Maple-Vail, USA

*This book is dedicated to the
process of conscious empowerment.*

Acknowledgements

This book has been several years in preparation and appears after many false starts. Whatever wisdom and understanding manifests through the medium of these pages owes much to the consciousness, perception and encouragement of Ríonach Bríd Aiken, who continues to explore this territory courageously with me.

Special thanks go to Charlotte Korbee, founder of the Shapers of Education International Foundation in the Netherlands. Her support and vision have enabled the Conscious Empowerment Initiative Facilitator Training that I lead to become a reality. Others who have significantly influenced my journey through their work or personal interaction are Abby Daniel, Daniela Cavallaro, Helen Barofka, Maureen Gillen, Monsignor Michael Buckley, Theresa Collins, Simon Treselyan, Carmel Long, Don Hanson, Maura Lundberg and Nicolas Guy Ngan. I also express my deep appreciation for Grethe H Hansen, Alexandra van der Hilst and Ken Masters, each of whom demonstrated their faith in me when I myself had none. Thanks also to John Hunt who turned up as my publisher just when he was needed and provided the impetus for me to complete the text.

I recognize that everyone is my teacher in some way, so there are many other people who have in some way contributed to this book, quite a few whose names I have forgotten. I wish to acknowledge here anyone who has ever been a part of my learning process, whether we were aware of it at the time or not.

I also have to thank the amazing presence of Sri Mata Amritanandamayi for the continued unconditional support she gives through the subtle realms as I continue my journey.

Personal Work

Altazar Rossiter is an intuitive channel, personal coach, facilitator and musician. He supports the ongoing development of *Spiritual Intelligence* through the experiential courses and in-depth trainings he leads in all of the processes described here as well as their extended application. He is also available for consultation, public workshops and talks.

He may be contacted through his website www.altazarrossiter.com or by email at support@altazarrossiter.com

Contents

1.
An Introduction to Spiritual Intelligence

All truth goes through three stages.
First it is ridiculed. Then it is violently
opposed. Finally it is accepted
as self-evident. SCHOPENHAUER

Spiritual Intelligence is a quality inherent in the process of being. It is not a theology, it is not religion nor is it religious; *Spiritual Intelligence* is not a philosophy, it is not a system of ethics or a moral code; *Spiritual Intelligence* is not simply inspiration or mere intuition. *Spiritual Intelligence* is none of these, yet it informs them all. But above all *Spiritual Intelligence* is not a rational intellectual faculty that can be brought to bear analytically or academically.

In a sense, because *Spiritual Intelligence* is an inherent quality of being it needs no developing. It simply is. It is humanity that requires development. This book is intended as a guide to discovering

Spiritual Intelligence for yourself. In that discovery process you will find yourself undergoing development. You will therefore also find this book contains lots of practical information and procedures to support that development and bring you along the road to self-empowerment.

I have always believed in possibility, especially the possibility that anything is possible. From as early as I can remember I kept bumping up against statements that human beings only use about five or ten per cent of their brain capability. (It's curiously coincidental that that's about the same percentage of the universe that can be seen or measured, which is not enough to support the coherence and behavior observed. Cosmologists now believe that *dark matter*, stuff that can't be seen or detected, accounts for the rest. They know it's there but they don't know what it is.) It seemed to me that if the other 90 – 95 per cent of our capability was there, it must be possible to connect with it in some conscious way. What, I wondered, if I could do that, and what would life be like when I did?

Everything in this book is a direct function of my own search for truth and the understanding I have developed for myself over the years that I've been working as a facilitator. In that time I've seen the devastation created by every kind of inhumanity that human beings perpetrate upon each other – war, violence, torture, abuse, judgment and criticism, shame and guilt – and the inhumanity we practice on ourselves. I've also been privileged to be part of the healing process in many cases. Most of this devastation is unseen, but its effects gnaw away at the fabric of our existence insidiously and continually.

For myself I now know there is an organic wisdom that we all carry, one that is constantly trying to inform us and support us. By *organic wisdom*, I mean an innate quality of knowing. This knowing appears at the strangest times, and sometimes runs counter to everything that makes sense, yet it is always appropriate. Even if I allow the possibility that my knowing is a delusion, and act as if the knowing is fully in alignment with universal truth, this wisdom continues to express and provide solutions. Such solutions are always better than I could have imagined or worked out beforehand. This is an everyday reality for me. I have come to regard this wisdom as *Spiritual Intelligence.*

The effects of apparently innate wisdom are increasingly recognized by science, although the ideas are not yet mainstream. Rupert Sheldrake is pioneering the concept of morphic resonance in biology; holistic practices like homoeopathy, acupuncture and acupressure are gradually infiltrating allopathic medicine; and quantum physicists like Amit Goswami are informing us more and more that the underlying substance of the entire universe is an interactive field of consciousness of which we are an integral part.

All of this is supportive of the idea of an expanded and inclusive reality informed by *Spiritual Intelligence.* This means that the fundamental existential scientific canon upon which we base our beliefs about ourselves is being revolutionized. The intellectual ground that supports the way we as humanity think about who we think we are is shifting beneath us. Change is upon us, whether we like it or not.

> *Spiritual Intelligence is a function of the mystery of the universe, one that underpins the existence of everything*

Essentially, some of the material presented here is an attempt to put words on the ineffable mystery of being. This is just not possible, by definition; but I believe it is possible to give an indication of how you can engage practically with the subtler aspects of yourself and it is also part of my intent in writing to facilitate this. The situations and processes described here are only truly understood through personal experience. Such experience comes in many ways; sometimes it is shared with others, sometimes it comes in solitude. However it comes, this experience is sacred to the individual. It cannot be reproduced in a book, although paradoxically reading can induce it.

As you evolve it is inevitable that you will discover places that are unique to you where you may disagree with someone else's perspective, including mine. This does not mean they've got it wrong, or that you have. It simply means that you've found an expression of your uniqueness, which is to be celebrated. Your challenge at these times will be to expand your understanding to recognize the validity of the other perspective, without invalidating yours. As you do this you are allowing more of your *Spiritual Intelligence* to surface, and, stepping into your own mastery.

It must be remembered that this book is not a definitive work. It is necessarily a product of my own personal journey and incorporates many of the lessons I've learned along the way. I am still learning these lessons and what appears in these pages is my best effort to interpret and translate them into a coherent text. It is my intention to pass on to you the insights I've gained so that you may gain your own. It is also my intention to give you the tools that I have used, so you can try them for yourself. Wherever you are on your journey I trust this book will serve you in some way.

Now a word of caution: Choosing to empower yourself and raise your consciousness through the exercise of your own *Spiritual Intelligence* is not an easy option. It's certainly not about escaping from the harsh realities of life. It is about valuing every part of yourself – especially your feelings. It demands ruthless honesty and the willingness to face your demons. There will be laughter and tears, delight and despair. But ultimately it's fun, and the rewards are joy, freedom, empowerment, independence and a degree of personal fulfillment that goes well beyond expectation.

COMMITMENT

Your commitment to yourself as Spirit is what really produces results. Only when this commitment is made can your Spirit commit to you, and that is when magic happens. Until you make this commitment you are unconsciously rejecting the greater part of yourself. This may seem like a criticism, but all it is really is a reminder of something you already know. If it feels uncomfortable then there's something here for you to take notice of.

This is the real subject of this book, and it cannot be stated too strongly. If you truly want to change your consciousness and fully embody as much of your authentic self as possible, it is imperative that you make it your intent to surrender your personal agenda for how things are supposed to be. This is not your agenda anyway, but something you have learned to define yourself by. Most of us are not ready to do this until we are well and truly sick and tired of our existence. It's when we are at the point of saying *No more of this, there's got to be a better way,* that we are at the edge of discovering something new about ourselves. The more attached you are to your comfort zone, and what looks like security the more difficult the initial step can be. When you are ready give up trying to exist with a minimum of discomfort, you are ready to live.

You must commit to living as truthfully as you are able, without worrying about how you can manage it. Just holding this as your intent will ensure that you continually find yourself in situations that challenge you to live more truthfully.

You must commit to listen to your heart, and to follow it when your head screams at you to do the opposite. You must be prepared to live with paradox and allow it to exist without finding a rational solution. You must be prepared to let go of anything you think you already know; because as soon as you decide you know a thing you close the door to any new way of understanding it. You must be ready to take the lid off some of the boxes you've kept tightly shut your entire life. You must be ready to go into unfamiliar and frightening territory. The curious thing about this is that when we get into this territory it's never as scary as it looked from the other (safe) side of the boundary fence.

I have evolved some very particular linguistic structures and procedures to access *Spiritual Intelligence,* and to help in aligning with it. These are made very clear in the text, and they may seem somewhat anachronistic. However they have evolved into their present form through the experience of their effectiveness. And just as I have evolved them I encourage you to do the same, but I also advise that to begin with you use them as I have given them.

The simplicity of these procedures belies their power. However that power is not inherent in the procedures themselves. It is the intrinsic power of your presence as it is accessed through them, and the key to this is your willingness to commit and surrender to your own process. This is what differentiates the procedures from techniques designed to produce a particular result.

TERMINOLOGY

Some of the basic terminology I use may be familiar in itself, but that does not necessarily mean that the way I use it is universal currency. In fact there is widespread inconsistency in the use of many of these terms, so it's important that I outline how I use them before you encounter them later in the text:

Ancestral Memory: the unconscious effects of family history, particularly the incidence of stigma, trauma, shame, guilt and blame that have been buried and forgotten. *Ancestral Memory* is sometimes referred to *Genetic*, or *Bloodline*, memory.

Body-Mind: the intelligence of the body to know what nourishes it, what causes harm, and when *Spiritual Intelligence* is trying to express. Kinesiology is the most widely known method for interrogating the body-mind.

Cellular Intelligence: an aspect of the body-mind that can be engaged in communication as a self-aware entity.

Cellular Memory: the memory of events, particularly trauma, held in the body long after mental and intellectual balance has been recovered. The cellular memory will trigger physical and emotional reactions, without warning, that originate with people and situations you may have moved on from years ago.

Chakra: a portal through which the physical body is influenced and energized by the subtle energy body, and the *Universal Field of Consciousness*. The seven major chakras lie along the line of the spine – root chakra at the base, second chakra in the sacrum, third chakra at the solar plexus, fourth chakra at the heart, fifth chakra at the throat, sixth chakra in the middle of the brow (third eye), seventh chakra at the crown of the head.

Consciousness: this is used in two ways, when it is capitalized (with an upper-case initial letter) it is a shortened form of the *Universal Field of Consciousness* or an aspect of it; without capitalization it represents the quality of self-awareness.

Consensus Reality: the world as we know it and participate with. This amounts to what is supported as truth by popular belief, conventional science and all of the institutions that form a particular culture. Consensus reality is never a static corpus although it may purport to be.

Divine Light: the energy of the *Universal Field of Consciousness* in its aspect of enlightenment and knowledge.

Divine Love: the energy of the *Universal Field of Consciousness* in its aspect of sensitivity and compassion.

Divine Truth: the energy of the *Universal Field of Consciousness* in its aspect of discernment and clarity.

Divine Wisdom: the energy of the *Universal Field of Consciousness* in its aspect of understanding.

Emotional Body: a part of the subtle energy body (aura or astral body) that holds emotional programming and is primarily connected through the second chakra.

Energy: the dynamic essence of spirit in action.

Essence of my Presence: the part of me that animates my body, that carries the energy of who I am into the physical realm. The *Essence of my Presence* is eternal, having many incarnations and living beyond my body. I also refer to this aspect of myself as my *Eternal Soul* or simply my *Essence*. It can be thought of as the *Higher Self*, but this concept implies a *lower self* that is somehow inferior and perpetuates the sense of separation, so I prefer to avoid it. *The essence of my being that holds the purity, love and wisdom of the Divine is what I call my soul. When I invite this to inform me it brings a sense of meaning, purpose and direction that supports and sustains all life.*

Guides: or *Spirit Guides*, are a non-embodied aspect of the *Universal Field of Consciousness* dedicated to support my physical self in aligning my worldly perspective with that of *Spirit*. *Spirit Guides* are also referred to as *Guardian Angels*.

Healing: coming to a place of balance within yourself, and acceptance of yourself, on all levels. *Healing* is a natural consequence of *self-empowerment*, but not its focus. It does not necessarily imply a cure for any condition, although cures are not precluded. It relates to *becoming whole,* which may not conform to any expectation of what that looks like.

Intent: the creative quality that modulates and directs energy.

Mental Body: a part of the subtle energy body (aura or astral body) that holds mental programming and is primarily connected through the third chakra. The emotional body and the mental body are generally under the control of the *mortal mind.*

Mortal Mind: the intelligence that rationalizes our existence and fuels the intellect creating structures, concepts and identities that define ourselves to ourselves; generally referred to as simply the mind, or the human mind. The *mortal mind* is a subset of *Universal Mind* but is largely unaware of this.

Self-Empowerment: the condition of being at one with your *Essence,* fully centered and present in your body. This condition corresponds to enlightenment and self-realization; it is being fully who you are at a cosmic and physical level. It is a condition that can be experienced fleetingly or for prolonged periods, and just because it appears it does not signify that the time to stop seeking has come. It is simply a sign that you are on the right road (for you).

Soul Memory: the effects of experiences from other lifetimes that can 'bleed' into this one, often held in place by vows and other subtle-energy devices. *Soul Memory* corresponds to what is known esoterically as the *Akashic Record.*

Spirit: the non-physical part of me that has existence beyond my physical perception, which can access all levels of wisdom as it ultimately merges into oneness with all that is. The term Spirit is used in dialogue as a shortened form of *Spiritual Intelligence,* or *the Intelligence of Spirit.*

Spiritual Body: a part of the subtle body (aura or astral body) that interfaces with the Soul and is primarily connected through the heart chakra.

The Highest Level of the Light: the place where pure intention, integrity and absolute truth reside, beyond the conceptualizations of right and wrong – often shortened simply to the *Light*.

Transformation: the process of changing the expression of your being so as to embody as much of the true essence of who you are as possible. This includes healing at all levels.

Universal Field of Consciousness: the entirety of creation, understood as a quantum field of energy holding the potential for an infinite variety of form and expression. This is known scientifically as the Quantum Vacuum, the Higgs Field, the Zero Point Field, or just the *Field*. In spiritual traditions it is God, the Web, the Weyrd, Great Spirit, Great Mystery, the One and the Source. It is also becoming known as the *Akashic Field*, and there are many other names given to it. Often it is shortened to the *Universe*, *Universal Consciousness* or *Universal Mind*. All other fields – and there are infinite possibilities – are a subset of the Universal Field of Consciousness.

Universal Law: the principles by which the flow and expression of energy are governed, and which allow the directive application of intent.

PRINCIPLES OF SELF-EMPOWERMENT

Using this terminology I've come up with a number of principles that I find allow *Spiritual Intelligence* to make itself more apparent. These have emerged over time through the practice of living as consciously as I can, and from considering my shifting perspective on the nature of reality. These principles are generative rather than prescriptive, by which I mean they are not absolute. There are many situations and ideas that will map onto them. I treat them as axiomatic but I encourage you to try them on and see how they fit.

My starting point is the fact that science seems to be discovering what has been a tenet of many spiritual traditions for thousands of years. If there is a universal field of consciousness that is the ground of all being – and quantum physics strongly suggests that there is, and if this field carries the energy trace of everything that happens – as it must, then this field must exist within, through and around us. We can only exist within it and because of it. It must be *in*-forming us all the time. This hypothesis gives rise to the fundamental principle of the interconnectedness of everything.

Some principles relate to the general implications of existence within the *Field*, some of them are specific to the inner process by which we evolve our level of consciousness. Also some of them may seem quite dense, complex or obscure. The main reason for this is that they have been inverted and distorted in the conventions that we live by. Don't worry if they take a little time to decipher, they are actually coded into you energetically but they have generally been misapplied or concealed by misapprehension. Unscrambling the misapplication is a task that the mortal mind is likely to resist at first. The mortal mind has after all been the instrument of interpretation so the idea of misapplication holds an inherent criticism – if these principles are right then the mind has been getting it wrong, for a long time. The entire construct of reality it has created for you to identify yourself within may be about to crumble. This is tantamount to self-annihilation, so resistance is natural.

You will find these principles threading their way through the book *in*-forming each other. In some places they will be identified in context as their relevance surfaces. In others they will remain implicit; to be internalized organically through the process of reading. They will weave an adaptive coherence without creating a rigid framework. There is no hierarchical significance to the order in which they appear. They are listed simply in the order that presented itself to me as I wrote them down. If this appears to have a natural flow please take that as an indication of the intelligence behind the writing.

The Principle of Interconnection

There is an infinite field of consciousness that comprises all of the energy in existence, from which all things arise. This *Field* is *Spirit,* although it is known by many names. All of creation is subtly interconnected through the *Field*. Despite appearances nothing is excluded. We are all part of the One, even though we form discrete packages through which the One expresses. This is the essential paradox that we embody.

This principle manifests itself through our sensitivity. We are all far more sensitive than has been realized or recognized. We feel the emotional resonances of the planet and all its inhabitants – some feel this more than others. Some don't know that they feel it. But what it means is that we need to develop clarity and discernment to allow us to differentiate our reactions from those of others around us. This is because our job is only to clean up our own reactive patterns; it is not possible to clean up anyone else's and it can be a major distraction to try. The natural consequence of clearing up our own reactions is that it becomes easier for others to clear theirs. The *Field* holds the revised information which others are then able to tune into and absorb...

The Principle of In-Formation and In-Tuition

The *Field* possesses its own intelligence, evidenced by its self-organizational ability to create coherent entities. Outside the rigor of 'science', this intelligence is known by various names that are rooted in mysticism including Universal Mind, Higher Intelligence, Divine Will and *Spiritual Intelligence*. At some point along the way this intelligence has informed all religions and spiritual practices known to man. It also seeks to inform me. When I integrate this information into my life I fulfill my potential and achieve my personal optimum expression in the world. This is never static, however. As the information held in the *Field* changes, so the potential for me to integrate anything that applies to me changes.

Spirit communicates to me via my internal senses (thought and imagination giving rise to *inner*-sight, *inner*-sound, *inner*-taste, *inner*-smell, *inner*-touch and particularly feeling), and also by reflecting my inner life back to me through my external world. This can be regarded as the phenomenology of my body and my body of affairs, the phenomenon of my own experience.

The more accurately I learn to read this *in*-formation the better I can control and balance my interaction with the world around me. I become independent and learn to trust my own authority. External systems have less influence on me and I am able to be more present with myself. Every experience has the potential to be my teacher if I ask my intuition to guide me in discerning the significance for myself.

The Principle of Universal Wisdom

Somewhere in the subtle realms of my being resides the knowledge that I exist within the field, and the field exists within me. This has to be as it is implicated in the organizational intelligence of the particles that make up my cells, and the cells that make up my body. Ultimately all of the substance that goes into my construction is part of the great infinite continuum of energy. Therefore all of the wisdom of the Universe lies within me and must be accessible with the appropriate key. This key is presence.

All I need to know is available to me in the moment I am fully present to myself. The information bubbles up from within and has no rational origin, although it may be possible to validate through the rational process. A great deal of time and attention is spent on formulating rational explanations for acting on intuitive wisdom and impulse in order to appease the cultural imperative of reason.

All I need to know is not necessarily the same as all I want to know. It is certainly not the same as all I want to know when I am distracted by fear, and emotional debris like that of resentment, worry, shame, blame, guilt and desire. These emotional reactions will always serve to blind me to the value of what presents itself to me as I need it. In fact, what I will want to know in such situations is *What have I got to do to make the emotion go away?* – which is unlikely to be what I need.

This principle implies that all the knowledge I will ever need is somehow already present within me. There is nothing for me to learn and nothing anyone can really teach me. What happens in my learning process is that the knowledge I need surfaces from within. The role of any teacher is therefore to draw this out of me rather than insert information into me. This principle coincides with the original meaning of the word *educare* (to draw out), which is the root of the English word *education*. There is a clear challenge to the conventional understanding of pedagogy (education, teaching and learning).

The Principle of Creation and Manifestation

I consciously connect with *Spirit* (the *Field*) by giving *intent*. This is ultimately via the realm of thought, but my intent is greatly amplified when I speak it aloud. Speech is a part of the physical reality I inhabit through the medium of my body, so the vibrations of the voice powered by the life force of the breath seed my intent into the physical realm.

The nature of the *Field* is that it is quiescent, yet pregnant with infinite possibilities, which it will manifest upon receiving the relevant instructions. It waits for our instructions. Our instructions take the form of setting and giving intent. This is a thought process by which we condition the aspect of the *Field* that is integral with our individual life form. Our thought creates a disturbance in the *field* that ripples outwards. The more focused intent we hold in this process the more creative (or destructive) force is harnessed to it.

The actuality is that the field is constantly manifesting the unconscious creations of scattered and unfocused intent. This begs the question as to what would happen if we became more conscious of our creative effect, and focused on clearing up the mess that we've created through our ignorance and *un*consciousness.

The Principle of Self-Identity (Principle of Subjectivity)

My self-identity is who I think I am, not who I am. It is what I've decided I'm supposed to be, or be like. It relates to what I've determined is necessary for my survival and any idealized manners I've adopted that bestow approval or credibility in my cultural setting. This is all artifice and pretense masquerading as truth.

One of the major talents of the human mind is its ability to make mental models and structures, and to notice patterns that fit these structures. This is how we make sense of ourselves to ourselves, and make sense of the world we live in. We gradually build up a context in which we position ourselves according to our interpretation of the circumstances of our lived experience. THIS IS NOT AN OBJECTIVE POSITION. Nor can it ever be for anyone, yet it is how we live and share our existence with those around us. In order for this to work it means that those around us MUST SHARE some of our interpretations of the general circumstances of existence. These shared interpretations engender a social order and become adopted as truth. They then govern what is *right* and what is *wrong*.

It is therefore more than probable that my mind has interpreted the circumstances of my incarnation from a place of confusion. Without any absolute terms of reference it has had to create a self-supporting model of reality that it can relate to. This has been done with due deference to its sensory input and the levels of anxiety present in me and my environment. There is no way to check the accuracy of any such reality model, all that is required for it to be adopted is that it seems to fit the available information. Consequently an identity will have been established that embodies any misapprehensions inherent in the original interpretation as dysfunctional psychological programs and patterns. These become ingrained and forgotten about, so they can be incredibly difficult to shift, but they are the foundation of who I think I am.

The Principle of Projection

My worldview is essentially a view of myself – and how I fit into the world I perceive around me. How I see this world is entirely dependent upon the identity I have assumed for myself. What I see will therefore always reinforce my self-identity. This means I constantly map my beliefs onto what I understand to be external to me. This is called projection.

Anything I detect that undermines or threatens the self-identity my mortal mind has created will be seen as detrimental to my existence. I cannot possibly accept that it relates to me in any way, so I will place it outside and separate from me. This includes any thoughts I have and observations I make about myself that fail to support my assumed self-identity. These thoughts are internalized as what I am not. I will attempt to attribute all of this stuff to someone or something else. In this way anything I reject in my external circumstances is in some way a reflection or a reminder of something I reject in myself. This is the mechanism of what is often referred to as the shadow.

The Principle of Projection sustains the condition of victim, and underwrites the process of blame by attributing responsibility outside myself. It is also fundamental to identifying my enemies (enemy patterning). For if I am right, what is wrong must exist outside me – where I do not exist, or in who I am not – mustn't it? What I am *not* can only exist where I am *not*. Anything that conflicts with my beliefs about myself and my world can then be displaced onto any aspect of my perceived reality that can be construed as the antithesis of my way of life. This was very neatly observed in Ambrose Bierce's *Devil's Dictionary*ª, which defines **infidel** as – "In New York, one who does not believe in the Christian religion; in Constantinople one who does." Attitudes seem to have shifted very little in the nearly one hundred years since this was first published.

The Principle of Reaction

Reaction is a fear response to anything that appears to threaten the notion of reality that I define myself around and participate with. Such a threat is effectively seen as a threat to my existence, as what I consider to be reality determines who I think I am. It is therefore associatively linked with the fight or flight survival mechanism.

My mind is capable of hi-jacking my feelings through the domain of fear – and more generally emotion – that operates through the subtle bodies, mental and emotional. This can cause me to feel responses to situations according to any dysfunctional psychological patterns and programs that I have structured my identity around. These responses are **reactive** and they include defensiveness, resentment, anger, jealousy, guilt, shame, blame, judgment, criticism, and deeply polarized behavior of all kinds. When I feel any of this it disconnects me from the communication of *Spirit*, which also presents through my feelings. It also distracts me from what is really going on.

My reaction is a defense mechanism that keeps my self-identity secure, and by inference it seems to keep me secure because my mortal mind thinks I am my self-identity. Once this process is understood every reaction becomes a tool for personal growth, because these can then be seen as signals that some misinterpretative process is running the show.

The Principle of Self-Awareness

My self-awareness permits me to be present with my experience. My self-awareness allows me to detach from the situations I find myself in, and observe my behavior as if I were my own witness. If I can be aware of this, even though I may be caught up in the intensity of the moment, I am on the way to being free of my reactive process. I have stayed connected with myself at a deeper subtler level. I am in effect my own master in this moment.

Any time I react unconsciously I engage with some dysfunctional program that I carry. My reaction reveals to me a wound that is yet to be healed, a belief that limits my expression, a part of myself that needs to be nurtured, loved and embraced. If I can find a way to dissolve my reaction I make myself more whole (healed). I reclaim a little bit more of who I truly am. This not only heals me, it changes the frequency of the vibration that I broadcast into the collective – *i.e. it changes the Field.*

The Principle of Responsibility

This principle is about being in a position to choose my response to an event or situation. Whenever I make someone else or some external situation responsible for what I feel, I have given my power away. I have effectively said: "You made me feel ... ..." If you examine these statements you'll see they are an affirmation of a belief that someone other than me is in control of my inner process. This is as true for what we regard as positive experiences as it is for the negative ones. Energetically there is no difference between saying, "You make me feel wonderful" or "It's all your fault." Either way I have disempowered myself voluntarily and unconsciously.

This is a curious reversal of what is widely accepted as the dynamics of our personal interactions. I will generally see myself as a victim of someone else's action rather than of my own interpretive process. This inversion is created by the illusion of transparency of our own interpretive process; we fail to notice the obscurity of our own mental constructions, because they are so effective at matching-up cause and effect on the basis of blame.

Most of the time I will actually want to see things backwards in this way, because the alternative would seem to be to take full responsibility myself. This could mean that I am responsible for inflicting all the pain and hardship I experience on myself. If that were true I would have to admit to getting things seriously wrong, which is tantamount to accepting blame.

The truth is that I may not be responsible for the pain and hardship, but I am responsible for how I respond to it. I am responsible for how I feel about myself in relation to it. And I am responsible for any associated process of denial that I practice.

The Principle of Separation

Any dysfunction I exhibit ultimately comes from seeing myself as isolated or disconnected from my core essence. It originates in the difference between what I feel is authentic for me and what I believe is the image of myself I have to project in order to survive. This split or difference unconsciously informs all my behavior, all my interactions and relationships.

Constant suppression of what I feel to be authentic for me is inherent in the process of creating a self-identity. It engenders a deep rage inside which will sabotage me if I do not find a way to allow it to express. If I do not learn to allow this expression it will turn inwards and fester as resentment. Thereafter, it will seek to escape and will express itself in destructive forms that are contaminated with resentment and all its cohorts: fear, bitterness, control, suspicion, jealousy, hate, judgment, criticism and blame...

The Principle of Approval

Approval is addictive, and this is because it has become a surrogate for the love that we deprived ourselves of without realizing what we were doing. The principle of approval is therefore one of the major devices of self-suppression.

From birth most of us are subjected to a barrage of programming that enlists us in the social order to which those who care for us already belong. This is structured around conventions of what is right and what is wrong. We are shown approval when we get something right, and disapproval when we get something wrong.

This is why there is a desperate need to be right – or to be seen to be right – in so many of us.

Because initially we cannot understand why anyone would be displeased with us – other than that there must be something deeply and intrinsically wrong with us – we interpret disapproval as rejection. We feel unloved, and this feels devastating. It sets up a belief that we are unlovable and don't deserve to be loved. In order to avoid the pain of this feeling we quickly begin to actively seek approval and orientate ourselves around the supply of this commodity. Over the years we learn to sacrifice every precious part of ourselves, our dreams and aspirations, in order to elicit approval from those we see as in positions of power and able to give us the approval we crave.

The Principle of Alignment

This is generally referred to as *the principle of free will*. What it means is that I have the freedom to explore anything I choose, but I have to accept the consequences of my actions. Alignment in this context means aligned with my soul's purpose, and for most of us this is the solution to the mystery of who we are that we are constantly seeking. But the soul will not reveal its purpose until we ask, and until we commit to being in alignment.

This doesn't mean we have to be in alignment one hundred per cent of the time. It means it must be our intent to be in alignment, and our commitment is to use our awareness to discern where we are out of alignment and make the necessary adjustments. We know when we are in alignment because we can feel it. It is a natural condition of centeredness, wellbeing, self-confidence, passion and gratitude. It is aliveness. In this condition we thrive and prosper, and although we may accomplish a great deal it will seem effortless.

If I find myself struggling to make something happen it's a sure sign that somewhere I'm out of alignment. All I have to do is notice this and hold the intent to make whatever shift is necessary to bring me into alignment. But I always have the freedom to dissent and continue with my willful struggle.

The Principle of Presence

When I am fully present to myself I am in a natural state of empowerment. When I am in this condition I am fully connected to the *Source*. Whatever I engage with in this state is fully aligned with my purpose, as nothing else will take my interest. In this state it is not possible for me to engage with a path unless I fully resonate with it.

Also, in this state, the invisible wounds that I carry can surface without fear or judgment. Their energy can then be re-absorbed into the continuum of the Universal Field of Consciousness. I sit with the feelings, fully present to them, allowing them to be there, and they evaporate. This self-healing process is effectively a positive feedback loop that enables me to be fully present more easily and more often.

> *Self-mastery cannot be avoided if you remain present with your experience and open up to the existential mystery of your being.*

PRACTICAL

It will be a feature of this book that each chapter will contain some practical process to assist you to open up to yourself. What is really important with all of these processes is that you let go of any preconception of what is supposed to happen. Simply give yourself the opportunity of experience and let it be whatever it is. Even the experience of "nothing" is valuable, especially once you begin to question what that nothing comprised of and what it felt like; it might surprise you.

You are unlikely to be aware of, or be able to connect with *Spiritual Intelligence* meaningfully unless you are able to bring yourself to a place of being present with yourself. This is not a condition we are taught at school or in any other aspect of conventional everyday life. We are far more likely to discover it for ourselves accidentally, but having no terms of reference for it, fail to regard it as significant. Consequently most of us need a bit of help and a bit of practice. The procedure given below is very simple, but very effective. I call it a centering exercise. Do it often.

> ➤ Sit (or stand) with your spine erect and both feet on the floor (crossing your legs limits the flow of your energy in your body). Imagine that there is a huge energy field, or aura, around you. This is your energy, your aura. It is as much you as the physical body you can see.
>
> Place your hands so that the fingertips of one touch the fingertips of the other one-for-one, including your thumbs. If it is possible close your eyes, but this is not essential. Then breathe deeply and fully, in and out, three times.
>
> With each in-breath imagine that you are drawing every part of your aura inside your skin, so that wherever your energy has been scattered it all comes back to you. If you can visualize this do so, otherwise just hold the concept in your mind as you breathe (this is using your intent) and it will happen even if you have trouble believing in it.
>
> Another way to do this is to think about bringing all of your attention inside your skin. By the time you take the third breath you will feel calmer and more together. Try it now.

This exercise is something that can be done in almost any situation to give yourself space. It takes very little time and almost nobody will notice what you are doing. I always teach it to people who have a stressful environment to cope with. If you have time and space lighting a candle, burning some incense and playing some gentle music can be added to the procedure. In later chapters I will offer suggestions for expanding this process.

2.

Conscious Intent

A truth that's told with bad intent —
Beats all the lies you can invent.

WILLIAM BLAKE

INTENT

The most powerful thing you can do for yourself is to set your intent consciously. Intent is the catalyst that enables energy to move and express as it is directed. When you set your intent you connect with the creative power of the universe, as it flows through you. Intent directly relates to purpose. It is deliberate. Intent creates the environment for an outcome to manifest. Intent is not about requesting; it is not about desiring; it is not about trying or wishing or hoping. Intent is not about wanting, although it is about having a sense of what you want even if you don't fully know what that is. Intent is about directing.

> *It is a universal truth that energy follows intent.*
> *Intent is the creative ingredient that modulates*
> *and directs energy.*

Intent is the initiating force for all change. It is where we begin any journey – by having an intent to get to a destination. We see and feel ourselves already *being* there, in spite of any fears to the contrary. Desire and need are also strong components that provide an impulse, but it is intent that moves us to action. This is the action of fully engaging the essence of yourself in the process of your life.

Conscious intent shifts us from quiescence to purpose, and gives meaning to what we do. Once we have set our intent it is only the self-sabotaging programs and beliefs we live by that can stop us from becoming what we set out to be.

The other side of this coin is that without conscious intent your energy operates without focus. The effect of this is that life seems to move at random. There is nothing to make it deliberate or purposeful. It can feel like you are simply drifting aimlessly, or being carried along by a tide of events beyond your control. Either way you are going nowhere. When you operate without intent you are switched off, disconnected from your power. Whatever you do without setting your intent you do unconsciously.

UNCONSCIOUSNESS

Unconsciousness is insidious because for the most part we are unconscious that we are unconscious. We know there is an unconscious part of us in operation from the work of Freud and the disciplines of psychology and psychoanalysis that he pioneered. And we know that it's like the submerged part of an iceberg, much larger than the part that can be seen above the surface. But we don't know what it contains, and the fear of what might be preserved in the ice keeps us from digging too deeply. Countless unconscious decisions can be lying dormant within us, many of which could be in conflict with the intent we are conscious of. Wherever such conflict exists there is likely to be an external manifestation of it somewhere in our lives.

Unconscious intent is one of the major sabotaging agencies that can undermine a creative outcome. Learning to recognize its presence is therefore an important step in reclaiming our power. This requires some discipline and dedication, but it's not as difficult as it might seem because we have our feelings to guide us. Our feelings are the key, because the mortal mind is governed by the unconscious routines that it's running. In this respect the mortal mind of reason, rationality and logic cannot be trusted. It will often conclude that a particular feeling is insignificant. This is a process of denial that can ultimately cause us to numb out a huge amount of our feeling capability, simply because we've decided it's insignificant and therefore can be ignored.

But the denial process can also be turned to a conscious advantage. The major indicators, or signifiers, of the presence of an unconscious intent are confusion, distraction, emotional reaction, and an inner decision to ignore a subtle feeling. This last item can manifest as forceful resistance. Therefore any time we find one or more of these turning up within us, we know we've found a part of the iceberg. We have an opportunity to know and understand ourselves at a deeper level, and to bring resolution to any associated woundedness. The signifiers of unconscious intent may present themselves singly, sequentially or together in any combination.

Confusion

Confusion causes us to send mixed messages into the *Field*. We may well be holding one thing as our conscious intent, but the unconscious may be holding several items that conflict with this. When this happens it feels like being caught in a bind, unable to make a decision. We know what we want all right, but we can't let ourselves commit to having it. In addition to this we will be unable to identify any particular reason why we can't commit; there will seem to be many. All of these reasons will be spurious, they will have no substance, but even when we see this we will still be unable to commit to the decision that will give us what we want or take us where we want to be.

This kind of confusion arises whenever there is a conflict between what we want to do now, and what we decided at one point in our lives we would never do. The chances are we made the 'never' decision in an emotional state, and as the emotional intensity faded we got on with life and forgot what we told ourselves in relation to it.

> Kate grew up in a violent household where her parents often came to blows. When she was a young woman she married a man who also turned out to be violent. Several years of suffering went by and eventually Kate left the marriage and got a divorce. There then followed a long period as a single woman, interspersed with relationships that lasted two or three years. Later in life Kate met a man that she wanted to marry, but because she had equated marriage with violence and made it her intent to stay single she couldn't allow herself to marry even though it was what she wanted. It was impossible for Kate to enter into a marriage until she recognized her earlier intent and changed it. Fortunately the presence of her irrational fear and the frequency of the obstacles to the wedding alerted her to the fact that something strange was going on, and with a little gentle inner exploration it was possible to see the origin of the conflict. Once this was understood and its impact felt Kate was able to move beyond her old wounds and the beliefs they had engendered.

Confusion undermines us in another way when we decide to do something, and soon after decide to do something else. Then a little further down the line we decide to take yet another direction. This looks like a failure to make up our minds, but it is really a failure to commit to ourselves and it is steeped in the fear of getting it wrong. Indecision makes it impossible for the universe to commit to us and the result is a fragmentation of our worldly affairs. The root cause of confusion is always an unconscious inner conflict. We are most likely to deal with it by denial – we pretend it's not there.

Distraction

This is similar to confusion. It demonstrates itself in the way we allow our attention to be captured by events and situations that have nothing to do with our aspirations or objectives. Some of these distractions will appear to be very attractive – even more attractive than what we originally set as our intent. In this case we revert to the confusion of being unable to choose what we really want for fear of making a wrong decision.

Other distractions take the form of imperatives. These are the debts and obligations that we believe are more important than our own needs. Our inner programming causes us to sacrifice ourselves, and our energies, producing frustration, regret, resentment and depression. We are imprinted with countless cultural programs and thought-forms that create an equivalence between selfishness and taking care of ourselves. Whatever we do that comes from a sense of duty rather than from a sense of generosity, or that comes from a sense of emptiness rather than fullness, is undermined by the inherent resentment of having neglected ourselves in the process. More of our life force energy is expended in keeping our true feelings and their residual reactions from expressing than in the flow of the action we have elected to take. The quality of any effort we put into the obligation is demeaned. Everyone loses.

Emotional Reaction

Fear is the primary inhibiter of any action: fear of what we might have to let go of, fear of who we might become, fear of judgment and criticism, fear of failing to match up to our own expectations and ideals. Fear will prevent us from setting any intent that is likely to take us out of our comfort zone. It will cause us to set our intent half-heartedly and set us up for failure. Interestingly, at some level we may be aware of this last possibility and if this is the case we will fear creating this experience for ourselves, so we can find ourselves in an unconscious double bind.

Fear generally lurks behind a whole pile of emotional reactions. The most obvious are anger, resentment and guilt, but it also figures in criticism, expectation, judgment, disappointment and it fuels humiliation, ridicule and shame which we will fear the experience of. So it causes us to suppress much of our true essence, which in turn builds up as frustration in one form or another and directs our own criticism inwards upon ourselves.

Denial of Feeling

This is the province of mental interference where the mortal mind overrides the voice of the heart. For most people the voice of the heart is a very quiet whisper, almost silent in fact. Whenever we set an intent that will nourish and support us, or bring us to a place of greater fulfillment, there is a feeling of excitement and joy that goes with it. Look for this in the area of your heart, and cherish it. It is a clear indicator that what you are giving intent for is in alignment with the essence of who you are. This feeling is soon swamped by fear and rationality. Once it has been swamped it is all too easy to pretend it was never there – to deny it – and to deny the sadness that goes with overriding it. This can cause us to cycle back through emotional reaction, distraction and confusion, producing a perpetual loop that takes a great deal of courage to step out of.

On the face of it these modes of what I'm calling unconsciousness may look as if they are major pitfalls to be avoided, and you can waste a lot of time and energy trying to avoid them. There are many strategies and techniques for this, some more successful than others. However what these strategies ultimately do is make the symptoms of the dysfunction disappear, creating the illusion that the dysfunction has gone as well. However, time and time again I come across people who have worked very hard at their strategies and techniques only to find that they eventually come up against their original condition anyway. And when this happens the crisis is often more intense.

A spiritually intelligent approach to these issues is to see them as a friend in disguise. The *principle of self-awareness* allows us to observe ourselves compassionately when we see our unconscious behavior surfacing. Recognizing when my unconscious programming is running the show is the first step to moving beyond it. I know that it is signifying to me that I have found something that wants to be healed. The next step is to relax and congratulate myself for spotting what's going on. I have found a key to the cycles I've been locked into by the past. What was unconscious is becoming conscious and I am then in a position to bring my intent to bear upon it, and heal it.

For the moment it is enough to see the possibility of this, and to feel it if you can. Later in the book there are suggestions for ways to initiate this process.

TAKING CONTROL

The conventional response to noticing our unconscious patterns is to try to take control. We look at what we've discovered and determine to abandon it. We try to force ourselves to behave in a way that we know is better, by which I mean a way that we approve of and one we know others will approve of.

Any attempt at this kind of control, however, is generally doomed to failure, as it is most frequently a tightening up process – one that locks in what needs to be expressed even more firmly. This normally comes from a state of wanting; a wanting things to be better. Because the current situation tends to equate to what is not wanted we start to define ourselves in terms of what is not wanted, without knowing what is. And wanting does not engage with intent.

Many of us go through life stuck in a kind of rut because of this, until some crisis jolts us out of it. Even then, because we have little conscious experience of the energy of our intent, it can be difficult to change effectively. What often happens is that we only succeed in changing one rut for another.

> I was thirty-seven years old, and in the prime of life. The trouble was I felt dead inside. Many times the idea had come to me to leave the house one morning, as if I was off to work, and just disappear, never to return. Furthermore, I'd been feeling like this for years and not realized what it was doing to me.
>
> My marriage had been flagging for a long time, and of course I had known this, but I pretended not to notice, as it was too

inconvenient to do something about it. It wasn't that I didn't love my wife. I had no passion for her, which was worse than not loving her. I felt guilty, and sorry for her for being with me. All I could do was make her miserable, something I appeared to be as expert in as she was at complaining about. Most of the time I was looking to see how I could create a bigger income so as to provide the compensations of a comfortable lifestyle. I had been effectively only working for the money for longer than I could remember, which was becoming progressively more difficult in every respect. What I had missed in all of this was how miserable I was making myself!

Everything came to a head when the industry in which I worked, went into one of its periodic slumps. The contract I was working on had a limited life. It was nearing completion and there was no chance of any further work for a long time. Much of the labor force had already been laid off, with nowhere to go. Suddenly I was faced with the prospect of being without the anaesthetizing effect of the diversions my income had provided. I hit a wall of depression. I was right on the edge of a total emotional and nervous breakdown, and my body was reflecting this back to me. I felt dreadful and I looked dreadful.

I hated my entire existence: my family responsibilities, my house, my lifestyle and the job I was now forced to cling to in order to sustain the status quo. And I hated myself for letting it all turn out the way it had. What was really depressing was the thought of endless years of the same thing stretching before me. If this was all there was going to be I knew then and there that I wanted no more of it. And I knew that there was only one person responsible for creating the situation I was in – me. I was at saturation and ready to blow.

So there I was with the accelerator flat on the floor. One-hundred-and-thirty miles-an-hour in the outside lane, furious with anyone who even looked as if they might pull out and make me slow down. Then I began thinking: I was insured, no-one would suffer if I wasn't around. The solid concrete walls of the motorway bridges looked almost comforting in their solidity as they raced past me. I could put an end to all of this right now. It would be easy. Undo the seat belt. Just a flick of the wheel and I'd tumble into oblivion.

I don't know why it didn't happen. I was right on the edge. But I heard myself saying out loud, "This is stupid. There's got to be a better way."

I don't know how many times I said this, but my foot came off the accelerator pedal and I was soon on the inside lane doing about forty, and getting in everybody's way because I was going so slowly. Thinking about it after the event, I reckon this was even more dangerous than flying down the fast lane as fast as my car would take me.

I pulled into the next service station, parked my car and settled myself with some coffee and a Danish pastry. Back to some semblance of normality. But something inside me had changed. I can feel it even now, many years later, in my chest, like a tingling feeling all around my heart and the area of my lungs. And I felt strangely unlike myself – unlike the self I had become, that is – but also more like myself than ever before. In that moment I could see all of the artificiality of the world I'd chosen to inhabit, and the inauthenticity I'd adopted in order to sustain myself there. And I was feeling the shock of realizing what I had been contemplating a few moments ago.

As I sat with my coffee and cake, it became my objective to deal with all my neuroses, my trauma and behavior patterns. I was sitting there on the knife-edge, shaking my head and saying softly, but aloud, to myself "I've got to sort myself out, I've got to sort myself out..." Anyone watching or listening would have agreed.

This was a major turning point in my life. This was where I actually committed myself to finding a resolution for all the emotional wounds of my past – all the stuff that I'd pretended didn't really matter, all the chaos and conflict inside me, the pain of my childhood and the invisible psychological abuse I'd suffered, the abusive and controlling behavior patterns I'd adopted as my own way of being in the world, all the stuff I was afraid for anyone else to know about. It became my intention to find my optimum state of being, and to express myself as authentically as I could in my life from now on. No more living lies!

This turned out to be easier said than done. Although things did begin to change from that point on, nothing happened overnight. I'd burned myself out trying to hold some kind of illusion together. I was hiding the mess of my life from myself, and from everyone else. I'd got myself so deep into despair it was to take years to dig myself out, with many tumbles on the way.

I don't even think it was my illusion I'd been holding, just bits of other people's I'd picked up as symbols of having things together and sorted. It was as if I'd just cobbled these together so it looked outwardly as if I was where they would like to be. It was sustained by one thing, the money I earned from the oil industry. Without a sufficient level of income the illusion collapsed, and there was nothing for it but to feel the pain I was really in.

In those days I had no idea about *Spiritual Intelligence*, subtle energies or the inner process. I was quite hostile to that "stuff", and certainly in denial of my own intrinsic spiritual nature. I didn't think anything had happened to me, other than I'd come to my senses at long last. Something had awakened within me, but it could have remained dormant just as easily.

Today I recognize the entire episode as massive heart-chakra activation, combined with a commitment to my own healing. I wasn't conscious of this at the time, but in that motorway service station I dedicated myself to my spiritual path, and began the process of my own healing. I'd given my intent, and I'd spoken it aloud. The ensuing year was one of the most difficult of my life.

I might have suddenly woken up to the issues before me, and seen them quite clearly in an intellectual fashion, but my old patterns were deeply imprinted into the cells of my body. I kept hearing the words, 'To thine own self be true,' echoing in my head, particularly when I was faced with some situation I'd habitually retreated from, or capitulated to, for the sake of a quiet life. One of my friends at that time even got angry with me, and asked me why I had to be so awkward. Why did I have to be different, why couldn't I be like everyone else? The answer was simple: to live the lie is the same as dying; it is not living at all. Needless to say, this person did not remain in my circle of friends.

Somehow the lid had come off the box I'd been living in. Instead of the artificial ceiling of the culture I'd grown up in, I could see the clear blue sky above. I hadn't worked out, yet, how I was going to get out of my box, but I knew I had to or die in the attempt. I was not about to let anyone put the lid back on. I didn't know then that I'd learned to put the lid on myself. It wasn't other people I needed to worry about, but my own self-sabotaging behavior.

GETTING OUT OF THE RUT

The content of my story is mine but its form is not unique. The initial experience of leaving the old rut behind is often intense. Major changes can occur in career, relationships and personal circumstances. All of which may give us the impression that we've made a fundamental shift in how we think, and even in how we identify ourselves. But after the furor has died down, and we reach a place of relative equilibrium, we can be left with the realization that there is still something missing from our lives. We think we're in a different play. However, the scenery may have changed, but the plot is largely the same. If this has happened to you, you'll know what I'm talking about.

The sense that something is missing stimulates a wanting based on lack. We perceive ourselves as lacking some essential item or commodity that would complete the picture for us if we had it. Such a perception is often what lies underneath the persistent longing for material gain, for the ideal relationship, or for some icon of success. Without intent your attention is drawn by what you think will provide these symbols, and you will be in a state of wanting; wanting whatever it is that you think you don't have that will provide you with a sense of fulfillment. And it has to be acknowledged that this can be the drive behind considerable personal achievement. But achievement is not the same thing as fulfillment. This mechanism causes us to seriously undervalue what we do achieve, because what we've achieved has failed to satisfy our deepest needs.

Setting your intent is not merely deciding what you want and going all out to get it. Setting a goal for yourself based on what you want is only to put your attention on what you think is missing, and that's the surest way to keep what you're really after out of reach.

There is a seemingly paradoxical concept here that needs to be expanded. If what you want is fulfillment, a sense of being complete in yourself, and you put your attention on what you think will provide you with this, what you will get is what you think will provide you with fulfillment NOT fulfillment. This is because you have focused your attention on what for you signifies fulfillment – the signifier is not the reality but only a representative for the reality, a substitute.

The psychology of this was observed by the twentieth-century French theorist Jacques Lacan[b], who used the term *objet à* as the signifier for the object of desire. Any signifier is an object in itself that cannot contain the essence of the object it represents simply because it is not that object. What is signified is only represented; it is not present. So when the object that constitutes the signifier is obtained what it signifies is discovered to be absent still. In this way what is desired continually slips away beyond reach, and is doomed to stay beyond reach.

> *It is a universal truth that whatever you put your attention on will somehow manifest in your life.*

Wanting

In the material world, people generally put their attention on what they want, but don't actually have. This modus operandi generally spills over into the realm of the abstract. We start to see qualities like joy, happiness and peace of mind as commodities that can be obtained like any other – often through some means of commercial exchange. These qualities are what are wanted, but what is pursued is something that it is believed will produce the desired condition, quality or experience. This is an area of huge misunderstanding and we are easily caught in this trap.

When we want something our real attention, our energy, is going on the wanting. So what we create is more wanting. This will never draw in what we actually want!

We also put our attention on what we fear, and this inevitably draws that to us. This is a demonstration of how we unconsciously allow our energy to run unharnessed through the realm of what we really do not want – worry, tension and anxiety. Think for a moment of how you talk about your life, your relationships, what you hope to create in your home, what you would like to experience, what you want to achieve in your work. How much of what you say is in terms of what you don't want? You might want to think about this, because it's important.

If you constantly say things like: *I want a job WITHOUT stress; I want a relationship that DOESN'T restrict me; I want a house that ISN'T always needing attention;* then you're putting your attention on what you don't want. Every time you use statements like this, to yourself or anyone else, you reinforce the energy around whatever it is you don't want and increase the chance of manifesting it. Most of us are quite accomplished in this area. This brings us to the concept of focus.

Focus

Focus is the act of holding a vision, holding a feeling, holding a sense of what you want to create. If you want to draw something into your life that you don't have you must focus on *having* it, rather than on not having it. Give intent to have the experience, feel what it would be like to have it, and go about your business as if you actually have it in your life. The *principle of creation and manifestation* operates this way. As your feeling aligns with your thought process you imprint the *Field* with the memory trace of having what you are focused on. The *Field* receives the instruction and sometime later manifests what you have created through setting your intent. When this happens the rut disappears.

CONNECTING WITH YOUR INTENT

You can only fully engage with your intent through a synthesis of thinking and feeling. To do this you must focus your attention on what you have chosen to experience. You must have a feeling for what this experience will give you, and allow yourself to feel it. Understand that this is a deep connection with yourself. Then you must commit yourself to whatever action is necessary to sustain that feeling.

To put it another way, you must engage your heart and allow this to supervise your mind. Any thought that weakens the feeling must be replaced with one that strengthens it.

It is a well-known fact that it is impossible to stop the mind thinking about something simply by telling yourself not to think about it. The most commonly used workshop example of this is to instruct people to think about pink elephants, and then tell them to stop that thought. The general experience is that people continue to think 'pink elephants' until that thought is replaced with another, for instance 'sunshine'.

So to support your shift in consciousness it can be useful to build up a library of thoughts that sustain the feeling of connection with yourself, and focus on these whenever something arises in you that causes the feeling to fade. These thoughts don't have to be elaborate to start with, they can be a memory of a particularly beautiful sunrise or a personal success that gave you a sense of fulfillment. Initially this practice can demand a degree of self-discipline that you're not used to, but you will find that holding your feeling in this way is actually very energizing. This is the key to manifesting your purpose in life. The next piece of the puzzle is surrender.

> ➤ I recommend that you stop reading for a little while at the end of this section, and take time to create at least one reference thought or vision for this library. Create more if you can, but one is essential. When you put the book down, place both feet on the floor if you can, arrange your body so that neither your legs nor your arms are crossed in any

way. Then close your eyes and go to the place where you
had the best, most joyful experience of your life so far. Relive
that experience in your mind as much as you can, recalling
colors, smells, sounds, anyone who was with you, what
you said, what was said to you. Remind yourself that this
actually happened so it was possible, and it's possible for
similar experiences to occur. When you have this feel it and
remember it. You are beginning to use your mind, rather than
have it use you. You are creating refuges for yourself where
you can retreat from the onslaught of your inner critic and the
emotional reactions triggered by that voice.

Refuse to listen to any internal suggestion that your
remembered experience didn't last or couldn't last, or that
what you're doing now is nonsense. This comes from the
aspect of the mortal mind that you cannot trust, so you must
ignore it. Some people find that they can tell this inner critic
to shut up, others find confronting it in that way makes it
worse. You have to find the way that works for you. (I know
that's not want you wanted to read.)

What I will tell you is that in my experience the best way
forward is kindness. The inner critic is a thought-form that
has evolved out of unkindness. It has learned how unkind
the world can be, so before it exposes you to the pain of that
it will be unkind from within. It will pour scorn on your every
attempt to open up to your sensitivity and give this part of
you any freedom of expression. Your inner critic will do this
not because it hates you – quite the reverse – but because
it fears the pain, criticism and humiliation that you will be
vulnerable to and it has developed this strategy to protect
you. Your inner critic loves you and it craves love in return.
Nevertheless it will continue to protect you out of its love
for you whether you love it in return or not. In effect it is an
aspect of unconditional self-love, because after all your inner
critic is a part of you. Respond to unkindness with kindness
and compassion.

SURRENDER

This is not so much letting go of what you *have unconsciously chosen to experience* [I use this form deliberately in place of 'what you want'], as a letting go of your agenda. This is where more work is needed with the mind, as the mind likes to figure things out. Once it has figured out how something is supposed to happen it has a tendency to reject anything that does not fit into the scheme it has created.

> *When working with* **Spiritual Intelligence** *the how of anything is generally irrelevant. It is a* **distraction** *that wastes energy and will defeat all outcomes that do not fit some preconceived model.*

It must be understood that the mind uses energy. Figuring things out, in the context of setting your intent and creating what you have chosen to experience out of your own strength, is a serious waste of your energy. The trouble with the mortal mind is that it thinks. It is used to thinking that it has to work out how to do everything, and then to drive you to manufacture the desired result. It thinks this because that's how we've learned to use it. We've been trained to do this through most of our educational life, and we've been rewarded for it in some way or other.

The chances are you received criticism when you failed to think as you were told, so it can seem dangerous and very frightening to stop this process. The *principle of approval* can kick in very strongly with a terror reaction when you embark on some project that hasn't been figured out. But the truth is, if you adhere to using your mind to control you out of what it thinks it knows you can only ever experience what you already know. You will never be open to anything novel or inspiring. Your mind may therefore need some de-educating.

What is very important to understand is that the mind has done, and is doing, nothing wrong. It has served you faithfully to ensure that you survive and thrive in the mental environment you've become accustomed to – your culture. It has in point of fact done its job brilliantly. And because it is brilliant, it can and will support you in your transformation. However for this to happen you must learn to stop criticizing yourself.

The mind has learned to respond very defensively to criticism. It has allocated this a priority associated with survival. So it just will not respond to any demand for change based on criticism or judgment. Therefore any time you reprimand yourself for the activity of your mind, your mind takes it personally and goes into protection mode.

The *principle of self-identity* dictates that because of the way we have learned to think, most of us have also learned to identify ourselves with our minds – our thoughts. A curious associative twist takes place in the unconscious in relation to this: if it's true that I am my mind, then it must be true that my mind is me. This is not the truth. It is, of course, the root of Descartes' famous pronouncement *cogito ergo sum*, I think therefore I am. It explains why you think you are your mind, and why your mind fears for your survival when it sees the interpretation of the world it has created for you coming under threat.

In its popularized form Descartes' theorem virtually denies the inherent spiritual nature of who we are. It is pretty much a total inversion of the truth of our being, which might be better expressed as *I am therefore I think*. You are neither your mind, nor your thoughts; you are much greater than either. The more you engage with your *Spiritual Intelligence* the clearer this will become.

Your mortal mind inherently believes in the rational Cartesian ethos, but it also wants to sustain you in the way that is best for you. The trouble is it thinks it is you (and you allow it to think this), so it wants to sustain itself along with what it has created as the best way to sustain you. These are not at all the same. Despite knowing all this, when you come up against the psychosis of the mortal mind's inversion of identity, it can be very tough to move through. The key to this is the *principle of presence*.

The mind commandeers the emotional body according to the *principle of reaction*. The mind creates beliefs, values and strategies in response to information available and circumstances that prevail at the time of individual incidents. These are valid in the moment, and may look like they fit various other situations, but they often become routines that cannot be questioned. This is especially the case with situations where we have been scared. In the case of trauma of any kind, such routines then become reactive patterns. When you operate through your reactions – your programming, you are no longer in control of yourself – your mind is. It is also to be expected that your reaction is a function of the past and is now redundant. It is also likely that your reaction no longer supports your best interest. Once the mind understands this it becomes easier for it to let go of its agendas. And that is what you want. This is the surrender that's needed for transformation to occur.

The mind's main function is to focus and refocus on your chosen experience, so you can sense, feel and see yourself having it. When you find yourself worrying about how to bring the experience about – or prevent an experience you don't want – you know that you are straying into distraction, and your thought process is becoming counter productive.

TRANSFORMATION THROUGH INTENT

The secret to all personal transformation is intent. We can only transform ourselves to the degree that our intent is engaged. The good news is that it's easier to engage our intent than it may seem initially.

The first step is to actually decide that transformation is what you want, and this is not such an easy decision to make as you might think. If you consider that transformation is the process of changing the expression of your being so as to embody as much of the true essence of who you are as possible (see chapter 1), you will realize that implicit in this process is the possibility that your whole world will change. It is a paradigm shift of immense proportion. Are you really ready to be all you can be and accept everything that entails? Are you really ready to take full responsibility for who you are? Do you feel the inherent empowerment that this will bring you, and is this what you want?

The truth is that very few of us are prepared for the shock that a fundamental change in the paradigms that structure our lives brings. Let's face it, it hurts. It hurts because so much of our identity is invested in our old ways. But when it hurts even more to continue living as we have been the possibility exists that the old paradigms have outworn their usefulness. The time has come to shift them out of our reality portfolio and invest our energies somewhere else. We can initiate this by consciously giving intent.

When I give conscious intent to be all that I can be I implicitly give intent to bring myself into alignment with my *Spiritual Intelligence*. This is the very essence of the *principle of in-formation and in-tuition*, which I choose to allow.

Inherent in this intent is a further intent to continually optimize this alignment in my unique way, as this is the nature of evolution. Once this compound intent is given – and it is given automatically in holding the intent to be all I can be – it is then necessary only to allow the mystery to unfold. The results are both subtle and profound, bringing a sustained increase in personal effectiveness to all aspects of life.

If this is what you want, the next step is to stop wanting and commit to the process. This means that you choose to do your best to be all you can be in all situations, and you make an agreement with yourself that you will do whatever it takes to sustain your commitment. This is the scary part, and the fear element is not to be underestimated.

In the very moment of making this agreement you engage your intent, and the chances are you will feel it somewhere inside your body, in the area of your heart. There is nothing wrong if you don't feel this, it merely means your intent has another way of signaling its engagement to you, which is yet to be revealed. However, the most common cause of feeling nothing is the self-numbing effect of continual denial of a subtle feeling.

> *Give intent for what you want to achieve.*
> *Commit to engaging with whatever is necessary to*
> *bring about this desire.*
> *Rest assured it will happen.*

> *How it will happen is not your business and trying*
> *to figure it out is a serious drain on your creative*
> *power.*

What is really important here is to remain open to possibilities, and pay attention to the subtlest changes and sensations in and around your body, as this is how you receive the signals from your non-physical aspects. There is a whole new language to be learned here, and if at first you don't recognize that something's been communicated all that signifies is that you're unused to the medium of communication.

Furthermore, in the very instant of making this commitment you are already doing your best to be all you can be, and this means your *Spiritual Intelligence* is already on-line even if you don't know it. From this moment on you will always be doing your best to be all you can be in all situations, and that best will be evolving.

When you commit to yourself in this way, whether you're aware of it or not, you send a clear compelling signal to your *Spiritual Intelligence* inviting it to join in partnership with your present understanding of your worldly expression. If you think about it you'll recognize that the entire process of committing to your transformation is an admission that you believe you've been under-expressing yourself. In its own way this is a powerful self-acknowledgement, and I don't mean this in the way of acknowledging your past mistakes!

I mean that when you do actually commit to your own transformation, you acknowledge the part of yourself that has been sitting in the background of your reality, virtually unnoticed. Now you are saying: 'I see there is much more to me than I thought; it's time I found out what is there – in the background; I'm going to explore who I am and be all that I am.' This is a major step in reclaiming your power. You have opened the door for non-physical and spiritual aspects of yourself to show themselves, even if you have no belief in them. You have already made a strategic shift, albeit unconsciously.

It's worth pointing out here that the best you can be will continue to get better, so when you look back over past events you may be tempted to think you could or should have done things better. This is a sometimes quite subtle, but nevertheless insidious excursion into self-criticism. It will only undermine your self-esteem to look at your life in this way. Realize that even when you may have been widely off in your discernment of the way forward you were doing the best you could in the circumstances, and these circumstances include your personal level of (un)consciousness. Compassion for yourself is vital, and it is not to be confused with self-pity.

Much will change in your life merely as a consequence of following the above process of giving intent. Things will be helped along, though, if you make conscious statements of your intent, and make this a regular practice. Such statements are best made aloud, so some preparation, and even ceremony, is helpful. This is a matter of individual preference. There are many ways of giving significance to your actions; they will all reinforce your intent. They will also serve to strengthen your connection with *Spiritual Intelligence*.

I recommend you borrow ideas from any ceremony or practice that appeals to you, but however you do this the most important thing is to give yourself the time that you need. Simple procedures like sitting quietly with yourself, lighting a candle and burning some incense are generally best. Find something that works for you and don't be afraid to change things around. Your ceremonies will need to evolve with you or they will become another millstone mindset that anchors you in the fear of getting it wrong.

PRACTICAL

Giving Intent

Now I'm going to give you a form of words to use to set your intent. This is a form I have developed over time, so I know it's not the only form that will work. However if you use this regularly things will begin to shift, and your *Spiritual Intelligence* will show you how to change the form to make it more effective for you. Taking a few minutes to articulate this aloud every day is in itself a significant step on your personal journey of transformation. The value of speaking aloud is explained in another chapter.

> ➤ I {insert name in current use}, incarnated as {insert full birth name}, call to me the infinite resource of all that I am under **Universal Law**; and I now give intent to remember and reclaim the sovereignty, integrity and mastery of my being and bodies as a Divine expression of **Universal Consciousness** in this incarnation. I call upon the **Essence of my Presence**, **my Guides** and the **Intelligence of Spirit** at the **Highest Level of the Light** to support and facilitate this process in me at every level, physical, emotional, mental and spiritual ... and I give thanks that this is so.

Mind Shifting

Another thing I encourage you to practice is mind-shifting; changing your thoughts at will. This is great practice at this stage because it can be regarded as playing.

> ➤ Go back to your library of thoughts that sustain your feeling of connection with yourself and give you refuge. (If you only have one, now is the time to create another). Now practice shifting from one to another. Keep your eyes closed for this and take your time. Remember to feel it. Quality is much more important than speed.

The next process you will find it useful to become adept at is controlling where you put your attention. There are two aspects of this skill I recommend for you to develop here, one internal and one external.

> ➤ With your eyes open simply allow your attention to fix on an object in your immediate environment, in the room or something you can see easily through a window. Look at it. See it. Focus your mind on it. Then shift your gaze to another object and do the same thing. Once you've really fixed on

a particular object **retrieve** your attention and move on. (Notice how you feel inside when you stop. What might the significance of this be for you?)

Next take yourself to your library of thoughts and rest your attention on one of your refuge images. Stay there a short while then fix your attention on an object you can see in the room. Stay with this for a short while, then move back to your refuge. Move your attention from inside to outside, and vice versa. Do this with your eyes open if you can and notice how it feels as your attention moves. What is your energy doing, where is it going? (It's good to ask yourself these questions and notice the answers you get.)

Have fun with these mind-shifting processes, see them as a game. It is essential to develop these skills when there is nothing riding on them. If you can exercise them at will you have a new tool to use when despair and depression start to creep in. Most people possess these skills to some degree, however they are by and large utilized unconsciously to distract and disconnect ourselves from the pain of life in general, rather than as tools of conscious intent.

3.
Language, Words and Power

"When I use a word", Humpty Dumpty said, in rather a scornful tone, "it means just what I choose it to mean — neither more nor less."

HUMPTY DUMPTY *in* THE ADVENTURES
OF ALICE IN WONDERLAND

Alignment with *Universal Consciousness* is a fundamental ingredient of the personal transformation process. The good news is that this alignment is a natural condition. We are naturally oriented to align with life, so the question isn't so much *How can we learn to do this?* as *What changes do we have to make in order for this to become the reality?* This is because much of the conditioning of the civilization we inhabit leads us to disconnect from nature, and also because our free will allows us to maintain a non-aligned existence if we can tolerate the pain and discomfort that go with it – *the principle of alignment.*

There have undoubtedly been individuals throughout human history who have been aligned, or able to develop themselves in alignment, and they have given us clues and left teachings on how we might do the same. One way or another such teachings have been reduced to words, a procedure haunted by omission that has led to the misinterpretation, misdirection and corruption of much of the wisdom. Much of this omission has been accidental, but there have also been deliberate attempts to sequester knowledge as a source of personal power. Either way these omissions collectively constitute a suppression that has evolved into institutions of dogma and control. Such organizations are still being spawned as cults and sects manifest in the spiritual void left by establishment institutions and the belief that we are not enough in ourselves.

In spite of all this we do still have the resources within to access the non-material realms for ourselves. We are able to align with the Zero Point Field and access the universal wisdom of *Spiritual Intelligence.* Indeed we are constantly accessing the non-material realms without realizing it. But to begin the alignment process we have to start looking in a different direction – we have to look within, rather than outside ourselves. We also need to abandon the idea that some all-saving benevolent external power is eventually going to rescue us from the misery of life, along with the notion that some objective paradise is waiting for us to walk into.

Primarily the resources we have consist of the non-material aspects of ourselves that we are conscious of, our thoughts and our feelings. These are the subjective components that color every action we take, whether or not we admit to it. Connecting with the feeling part of ourselves accesses the creative energy of our intent; speaking aloud translates the subtle energies of the universe into physical reality. These two facilities together constitute a formidable instrument of self-empowerment. When we make the intent to align with *Universal Consciousness* in such a way as to allow *Spiritual Intelligence* to inform us, and then speak this intent aloud, the alignment happens instantly. We empower ourselves with our own intent.

CONVENTIONS OF MEANING

Understanding what meaning is about has been, and still is the subject of much philosophical debate. Little of this is relevant to this book, but some consideration is necessary as meaning is closely related to intent – and intent is relevant. This is especially the case with the words we use.

Words are such an everyday commodity that their existence and function is largely overlooked. Mostly they rise up in us unnoticed and we voice them without thinking very much. Occasionally we are frustrated because we can't remember or find a word to correspond with the concept or feeling we want to express. But few of us stop to consider the function of our words; we say them with an unconscious assumption that they are transparent and mean what we say.

It is traditionally accepted that words actually mean something, but this is a convention. The artifice of this is reflected in *A Course in Miracles*[c] where lesson one of the workbook begins with the affirmation: "Nothing I see ... means anything." Words are given meaning by those speaking and hearing them, and these meanings are not necessarily concurrent.

Let me state here and now that there is no absolute authority of meaning inherent in any word. All words are representatives only – signifiers – of something else. They represent things, concepts and actions, and it is mostly forgotten that they are things in themselves.

> *What anything means to you is a function of*
> *your personal interpretation. There is no reason to*
> *expect this to be relevant to anyone else.*

In the oral traditions that have been the mainstay of most natural and aboriginal philosophies – it's actually quite interesting to notice how the principles of many of these broadly agree – there are three levels of meaning ascribed to spoken words. First there is the literal meaning where *a rock* means just that, a single piece of rough stone. Then there is the metaphorical meaning where *a rock* might be seen as representing something or someone who displays strength and solidity. Lastly there is the archetypal (or universal) meaning where *a rock* is seen as representing an inherent quality and applied to any person or thing that exhibits the qualities associated with a rock.

Our over-familiarity with the standard concepts of meaning current in our society causes us to neglect the possibility of the presence of anything else of significance. With the ascendancy of the printed word in all forms of intellectual interaction the traditional levels of meaning have been marginalized, surviving only in analytical academic contexts. This amounts to a level of unconsciousness that characterizes westernized society as a whole.

It is a fact that all levels of meaning are potentially present at any one time. It is our intent that determines which level we project into the universe when we speak, and our conditioning that determines our interpretation of what we hear or see. However because of our necessity to engage with the physical realm we tend to interpret at the first level of meaning – the literal, but it must be remembered that the universe always communicates to us at the third level. This means that the messages from *Spirit* are coded a bit like crossword clues. It is up to us to decode the meaning for ourselves, and turn this into words if we so desire. You may be beginning to think that this is a process you need to be more conscious of in yourself.

THE POWER OF WORDS

It is widely accepted that words have power, but if they are merely representatives for something else and have no inherent meaning how can this be so? Despite their lack of inherent meaning, words do carry energy and this is what we're interested in. You can begin to understand this by considering another question: *If words have power, where does that power come from?*

The power of words, and the language we use, in creating the reality we live in has a long tradition shrouded in mystery. But few truly appreciate how this happens, and why we don't always seem to be able to create the reality we want. Most people in the "Christian" west are familiar with the opening words of the Gospel of St John:

In the beginning was the Word, and the Word was with God, and the Word was God (John 1:1). This can be quite enigmatic until we look at some other spiritual traditions. In creation stories as diverse as Hindu, where OM is the sound of creation, and the Native American Hopi sound is the essential element.

It would seem then that it is not simply words but the sound of their intonation that carries their power. We might then consider how we affect our reality if the sound of a word is conditioned by the intent with which it is uttered.

> *Choose your words with care.*
> *Consider that everything you say contributes*
> *to the energy of the environment you live in.*

So to return to the question I asked earlier: *If words have power, where does that power come from?* The answer is that, if you are speaking, the power comes from you. It is your power that is being expressed. And if this is the case then it's a good idea to ensure that any energy you put into the speaking venture affirms and supports your life process. What you say is fundamental to the way you exist in the world, because your word is quite literally your bond.

Rather than say words have power it might be more appropriate to say that words are instruments of power, especially when spoken aloud. It is the significance of this that is overlooked in our everyday use of words in conversation.

Words are one of the most powerful transformational tools we have at our disposal. By speaking our intent we can create energetic shifts in the entire expression of our being. We can work with ourselves, and with others, to bring peace and harmony into our lives. This is the ancient secret of invocation and incantation that has been obscured by the spin of history, the self-seeking quest for power and political expediency. But it is a secret you can learn for yourself. It is therefore really valuable to develop an understanding of this process, and raise your level of awareness in relation to it.

We can reach into the cellular memory, into the ancestral memory and even into the soul memory to redress the balance of ancient wounds. We can address other lifetimes in the here and now, especially where these have a relevance to current issues. We can shift our relationships to a new level. We can bring closure to situations that years of therapy have failed to resolve. We can do all of this, and more, because words are an inter-dimensional portal through which the non-material energy of *Universal Consciousness* can take physical form.

RECLAIMING YOUR OWN POWER

The written word is read by a process of dynamic observation and interpretation, which largely rests upon seeing it. If it's true that nothing I see means anything, then words on the page, of themselves, mean nothing. This begs the question of where the meaning comes from. The answer to this must be the reader; there is nowhere else for it to come from. Words are given meaning in the moment of reading by the person reading them. So whenever you say *this means ...* , *that means ...* or *it means ...* you are articulating an error that masks the truth that *you* are assigning meaning to what you see or read.

Underneath this truth is the fact that it's your energy that produces the meaning, so it is your meaning. The same words could have quite a different meaning for another person. However, we like to believe that the meaning remains fixed. We expect the meaning of our words to be understood by another in *exactly* the same way that we understand it. This is neither likely nor reasonable, yet we can be very attached to this as a principle of the lives we lead. This is what provides the legal profession with a very good living.

It is by this very process of attachment and expectation that we transfer our power to external sources. We give our power away without realizing what's happening. It is an everyday process endemic to the culture we live in. We do it with objects, and we do it with people. The *principle of projection* is in operation here mapping our interpretation of a situation onto an external entity, and fitting this into our personal context of what makes sense.

> *Projection self-programmes you to believe that the*
> *source (or locus) of your power is outside yourself*
> *– but it is only there because that's where **you** have*
> *placed it.*

When we say somebody means something we assume (make an *ass* out of yo*u* and *me*) that our interpretations match. Then we identify any reaction we have as being their fault. What they said made us angry, sad, laugh, sorry, happy, and so on. We have made them responsible for our experience. We have *projected* our power onto an external agency. This is something we do all the time.

Perhaps the commonest example of this is the way we use language to explain what we read. We say: *it says here, the book says* or *it says in the paper* and so on, forgetting that the book or the paper cannot *say* anything. We readily understand this metaphor but through it we create an inversion that determines us in the position of listeners. At the literal level of meaning we accept this, but what have we heard? It is us who have the ability to say, any text is a mere representation of living speech.

Projection is self-sustaining; it inverts the truth and supports victim consciousness. It sustains the illusion that you are not responsible, and undermines your confidence and self-trust. A way around this might be to think in terms of what something means for you, and to own any meaning as your interpretation – because that's what it is. When you do this you retain your energy. Another useful exercise is to watch out for any time you use a form of expression that projects the ability to say onto something that could never physically say anything, i.e. *what does the book say?* See if you can find another way of articulating that keeps the locus of power within you.

It can be very interesting to try this out and see how it actually feels inside when you do it. You will be reclaiming your power, which can trigger a lot of fear. So if you find yourself resistant to the idea of changing your thought process – and how you express it in words – you might want to consider what you could be afraid of, and what are the advantages of giving your power to someone else. Becoming conscious of this is in itself a significant step.

Another way of disempowering ourselves that is very prevalent in so-called new age spiritual thinking is to hide our desires and disappointments behind the concept of what was 'meant to be'. Desires and disappointments are the well-known symptoms of that unspiritual quality attachment, so we mustn't be seen to suffer from it if we are spiritually evolved. All too often when we miss out on something we wanted, we write it off by telling ourselves something like *"I guess it wasn't meant to be."* This could, of course, be true. But we undermine ourselves if we consistently adopt this position. There is an implied surrender to higher intelligence in statements like this, but what they are really saying is that *I have no control over my life, nor do I have any right to expect any.* If you pay close attention you will hear the sighs of self-pity echoing in the *wasn't meant to be* phrase clearly signaling a state of victim. Similarly, the smirk of self-satisfaction often lurks behind the *was meant to be* phrase. We can learn a lot more about our situation if we consider the mixed messages we give the Universe in the words we speak.

Pay attention to the expressions you use to hide behind. See if you can catch yourself feeling one thing and saying another. Whatever you say to the world in general you say to yourself. Your body hears, and it knows when you tell a lie. This sets up a tension that can undermine everything you attempt in life, as your body develops a lack of trust in what you say. This kind of tension is what lies underneath much of the stress experienced in modern life. A conflict is set up between what is felt and really needs to be expressed, and the actual expression that comes out in a form designed to appease the environmental circumstances.

MOVING BETWEEN DIMENSIONS

I use the term *dimensions* here to indicate a difference in the spaces where what we consider to be physical reality and non-physical phenomena exist. It is not widely acknowledged, but speech can be considered as a tool that we use to move our consciousness between dimensions. To understand this it is necessary to understand speech as a vehicle for the expression of thought. Nobody has yet defined where our thoughts exist, except to say that they are located somewhere in the mind – the mind being the place where thoughts exist. But where is the mind? The notion that the mind is simply lodged somewhere in the brain is an assumption that has yet to be proved. An increasing number of scientists are beginning to recognize that it may extend into a field, or be part of a field.

Wherever it is that thoughts exist, it lies outside the space-time continuum of what we consider to be normal reality. So it may not even be a place at all, in the way we normally understand the term place. Yet there is no doubt that thoughts are a part of the reality that we inhabit. They are things of our experience. They exist, but they are abstract, or non-physical. We perceive them inwardly. Just try a little experiment for yourself here.

> 〰 Close your eyes and let your thoughts be whatever they will. Now reach out a hand to wherever it is you see, hear or think your thoughts. It may be that your hand went to your head or some other part of your body. It may be that your hand went to a place outside your body. It may be that the place is not consistent, that is not always the same place. There's no right answer to this, but it's something few of us ever consider. You might also try putting your hand, or pointing to, where your consciousness resides. Allow yourself to be present with what you find, and consider if it holds any meaning for you.

In contrast with thoughts, words do exist within the space-time continuum. They are a part of our physical reality. And broadly speaking we experience them in one of two ways. One is through the speech process, talking and listening. The other is through reading and writing.

For now it is the speaking process that interests us. The physics of speech roots us firmly in the physical world. Sound is a physical phenomenon. It's not something that we can grab hold of with our hands, but neither is it abstract. It is a pressure wave, something that has a physical presence. It can be measured. It is also a vibration that we can feel with our bodies, our skin and bones – this is how we detect it. In this respect it is time based, as vibrations have a frequency; and it has magnitude, which requires space.

Although we might think of our voices as the source of sound within us, we actually produce sound from our voices with our breath. The breath is also the carrier of the life force into our bodies, so our speech is imbued with the living energy of our being. Perhaps it is no surprise that the spoken tradition is widely regarded as the primary manner in which knowledge is passed down through the generations.

If thought exists in one dimension and speech in another, when we turn thoughts into speech, or speech into thoughts, we are moving our *consciousness* between dimensions. We are moving between a subtle reality and a physical one.

> *When we speak aloud we bridge dimensions and engage the creativity of the universal energy of our life force.*

WORDS AS TOOLS OF TRANSFORMATION

We have come to think of words primarily as a means of communication. However, as you will see, this is largely a delusion. What we do with words is anything but communicate.

Words are used to control and manipulate, to blame and to shame. We use them to impress and suppress, to get what we want and to avoid what we don't want. We use them to say one thing when we mean another. We use them to divert attention away from our mistakes. We use them to obscure the truth. We hide behind them and we use them to excuse and justify our self-identity. And we use them to deny what was generally understood from what we said in the first place – in current jargon to *spin*.

} *When you say one thing, you always **potentially***
} *imply another by omission.*

Whatever we think we're doing with words however, whenever we speak them we are participating in an act of creation. And if this is the case it is an opportunity to create something different in our reality. We can think of the reality we want to create, speak the words that describe it and feel what the vibration does to us inside. We are not merely communicating with other people, we are communicating with unseen aspects of ourselves. Also when we express our ideas and visions through speaking aloud we not only open a trans-dimensional portal within ourselves, the potential for a similar opening is created in anybody else who hears us.

This makes language a key factor in our self-awareness, and our self-empowerment. It is an extraordinary access way into the non-material realms of our existence, one that masquerades as an everyday feature of living. For when we speak our intent aloud every cell in the body 'hears' through the physical vibration created which resonates throughout the body. When we speak our intent aloud, not only do we bridge between dimensions, every cell in the body knows we mean business and responds. Once we begin to understand this, we can learn to use it as an instrument of self-transformation. But first we have to address another aspect of ourselves that has consistently been suppressed – our feeling self, because our feelings are a major part of the transformational toolkit.

ACCESSING SPIRITUAL INTELLIGENCE

The major drawback with language, as we generally practice it, is that we use it to make sense of things. That is to say, its rules and structure encourage rationality. A good thing too, you might think, and so it is. But the process of rationalizing is often the enemy of feelings, and feelings offer another primary doorway into the non-physical aspects of ourselves.

> *Significant celestial bodies, stars and planets have been*
> *discovered by observing small, almost imperceptible*
> *disturbances in the motion of neighbouring planets*
> *and stars. Some of our feelings are small, almost*
> *imperceptible sensations/disturbances in the body*
> *– these may well indicate the presence of something*
> *significant that we haven't known how to look for so*
> *assumed wasn't there ...*

Just like thoughts, feelings are abstract. We can't simply grab hold of them and examine them under the light, as we might some physical object that interests us. We perceive them inwardly and assume they are within us. This is not always the case, as I will explain later. But unlike thought, which is perceived with the mind, we perceive feelings with our bodies. And we have learned to ignore our bodies until they force us to pay attention by the development of disease. Even then we do our best to suppress the disease by medical treatments that treat the body as a machine that has inconveniently broken down. However, our bodies are just not reasonable; they operate with a different level of intelligence. The failure to acknowledge this is the root of a huge amount of conflict in our everyday reality.

For something like two-and-half thousand years Western culture has been biased in favor of the rational. The mind has been privileged, and respected, above the body. Feelings have been dismissed as irrelevant and overridden.

The supremacy of rationality is upheld simply by excluding what cannot be rationalized and regarding it as insignificant. The rules of reason are assumed to be applicable to everything, whether they fit or not. So what cannot fit in with these rules – anything that does not make good reasonable sense – is immediately disqualified. By its own self-sustaining circular logic, reason has triumphed over that which cannot be articulated.

Through this means feelings have been systematically subjected to the process of denial – they don't fit in with the rules for making sense; therefore they must be irrelevant and can be ignored. This has become a cultural ethos, epitomized in the English 'stiff upper lip', creating tension and severe emotional stress.

This is a major affliction for men in modern society. Concepts of gender are another area where there has been a revolution in intellectual thought over the last half century, but the changes in understanding are taking a long time to filter through into physical reality. Sensitivity of feeling has long been seen as the enemy of the male imperative, which is to take any and all necessary action for survival. Once a man starts to feel, to empathize, he's not going to be able to kill his enemy and keep himself and his family safe.

Some years ago I ran an informal weekly group-healing seminar. A young man in his thirties, Jonathan, regularly attended these meetings. He was from an agricultural background where physical strength and hard work were prized qualities in a man. Jonathan demonstrated these qualities admirably, but there was more inside him and he wanted to know what that was.

Because of the inherent spiritual nature of the meetings Jonathan felt he had to keep his attendance at them from the rest of his family with whom he shared a business, as he knew he would be subject to ridicule if they knew. It transpired that for some time he'd been suffering from serious back pain, and his family had been deriding him for being the weakling of the bunch. As the weeks went by Jonathan's back pain got worse and he became unable to do his work, which he simply described as very strenuous.

Eventually he came out with the fact that he hated his work, and never wanted to return to it. After a little gentle coaxing he told us the story of how he would spend his days in the forest feeling totally connected with the wonder of nature around him. He loved the trees and he knew he would never have been able to share this with anyone in his family. As he told us this he began to weep. He then went on to tell us that he'd been given the job of cutting the trees down. Every time he used his chain-saw he felt devastating guilt, shame and remorse, and the pain in his back was excruciating.

Seemingly by coincidence his back pain had started when he

had been given this job. He explained the pain to himself as being caused by working in a lop-sided unbalanced way that put a strain on his spine. Gradually he realized the imbalance wasn't just physical, but a physical reflection of his inner condition. Jonathan decided to leave the family business and his pain disappeared the day he did.

Jonathan is an example of a man who just did not know how to deal with his sensitivity in a society that demanded he have none. He had a lot of difficulty equating his quality of sensitivity with the fact of his manhood. The notion of the incompatibility of these attributes was ingrained in him through generations of hardship. Ultimately he experienced a physical breakdown, which enabled him to make an emotional and spiritual breakthrough.

Much Eastern philosophy has in many ways produced a similar suppression of feelings. Many respected spiritual authorities teach their disciples to focus not on the material aspects of life but on the non-material, the ineffable. As the body is material, through a process of association it soon becomes regarded as representative of the material state, which is already defined as unimportant in relation to the spiritual. Consequently whatever happens within the body is also regarded as unimportant. This results in the suppression of feelings, or denial, as the body is the seat of our feelings.

This is a dis-ease of the spirit that creates a predisposition to abuse of the body. The disaster in all of this is that the process of denial causes us to forget how to feel. When this happens we become, not only distanced, but cut off from the non-physical dimension that is accessed through our feelings.

Because the feelings are just that, an indication in the physical of the non-physical, they also offer an access way into the subtle realms of our existence. When the mind is used in support of this, rather than to override it, we begin to access, not just emotional intelligence, but *Spiritual Intelligence*. By contrast, when the mind is used to undermine the feelings by rationalizing them we effectively block any possibility of spiritually intelligent expression.

FREEING YOURSELF FROM THE IMPRINT OF CONDITIONING

The imprint of conditioning has many threads and strands that we will be exploring in more depth as we proceed through this book. What has to be understood is that because conditioning is mostly a function of the intellectual mortal mind, mental strategies have a limited use in dealing with it. We need a different level of intelligence, one that is independent of what we know intellectually and we have to give it permission to arise in us.

In order for this intelligence to surface, and to engage with your own transformation it is necessary to re-assess and possibly repair your relationship with the more subtle aspects of yourself. It is to be understood that every thought and every feeling you have has some relevance to who you are and where you are in life. These subtle fleeting thoughts and feelings carry the information you need to begin reclaiming who you truly are.

The major difficulty in this is presented through the *principle of self-identity* (see chapter one). Because of the conditioning of our various circumstances, our thoughts and feelings have been given certain values that we have learned to identify with. This conditioning does not define who we are even though we may believe quite strongly that it does. Furthermore we have been confused by the conflicts that have arisen between thoughts and feelings, and anywhere that we have allowed the one to override the other. Because of all this it is more than likely that you are not who you think you are, and much of your work in a personal development sense is to move beyond your conditioning.

Engaging with these concepts is nothing less than an adventure in consciousness. It is the journey of life and it cannot therefore be accomplished over night. (You should beware of anyone who tells you it can be.) It is a journey into the unknown, full of excitement and an accompanying measure of fear to walk through. There is no map of the territory to be covered simply because you are a unique individual and your map would be no good to anyone else. Neither would anyone else's map take you where you need to go, although it may look as if it will. Also there is no clear destination in relation to this journey.

The paradox in this is that you will find sharing the journey with others a great support. Each step on the way will bring you closer to a true self-awareness, but that awareness will be continually expanding so you will continue to exceed what you once thought possible. This is another reason why the intellect is a poor guide; it will only allow you to aim at what it can conceive of through its imprinted conditioning. Much that you once would have thought impossible about yourself will become commonplace to you. I express it in this way because the conditioning mind-sets you set out with could not allow you to conceive of yourself as you will be as a consequence of connecting with your *Spiritual Intelligence*.

There is something about the mortal mind to be made clear here. Your mind is not your enemy. It has been intent on keeping you safe as it figured out what you needed to survive. It has done this job very well through the creation of strategies, patterns and routines that it runs virtually unconsciously, and which fit your perceived circumstances. What has happened in that process of developing your behavior patterns is that it has created a situation that only allows certain kinds of thoughts to be entertained – those that are legitimized by the social order and its dominant ideological paradigms. Thinking is not a problem; it's what is being thought and how that limits us that create the difficulty.

Right now would be a good time to consider your thoughts and feelings in this moment. There is nothing to do but allow whatever is present to be there. This is the *principle of self-awareness* in practice: just allow whatever is present without any judgment – even if it is judgment or criticism that's present. Even if you think there's nothing going on inside you see if you can describe that nothing to yourself. As you become more conscious of the subtleties of feeling and thought that you ignore and override in your routines of convention you are empowering *Spiritual Intelligence* in yourself.

Now consider if there's stuff going on inside you – thoughts, pictures, sounds, feelings, nothing – who is it that's experiencing all of that, and who is it that's watching it? Which one is really you?

Becoming aware of this "split" may be a little disconcerting; it may be something you'd noticed before and refused to allow yourself to dwell upon. See how long you can stay with it. You are not in danger of becoming schizophrenic if you can see this in yourself; you are actually functioning through the *principle of presence*. If you can be aware of this split you are on the way to recognizing your true self: make it a practice.

To assist this process you can use the power of your voice and breath to give intent for it. Make sure you're in a quiet space where you will be undisturbed; center yourself using the procedure given in chapter one; then say the following aloud:

> ➤ Spirit, please work with me on every level, physical, emotional, mental and spiritual and help me to notice anything that is ready for me to address in this moment. Show me where it comes from; bless it with Love; neutralize its effects and release me from its influence. And do this for me now!

> { *A major gateway between the physical and non-*
> { *physical realms is created when we speak our*
> { *intent aloud.*

You may like to make a note in the margin, or in a notebook, of anything that comes up as a consequence of this. This will give you some ideas about the areas you might need to focus on in your journey. Later in the book I'll be giving you more practical structures to frame your intent, which will help you interpret the subtler aspects of yourself in new ways. I'll also be giving guidance on working with the various issues that will come up, but for now it's really important to accept anything going on within and watch where you want to reject it.

As you progress further through this book you'll be looking at how you can use your voiced intent to facilitate your growth. Fundamental to all of this is an understanding of the energy and the power of your own vocal expression. It will be called upon more and more to support your growth.

PRACTICAL

Whenever I work with *Spirit* I like to set up a sacred space for the process. I always do this by speaking my intent aloud, using an extension of the form for giving intent shown in chapter one:

> ➤ I {insert name in current use}, incarnated as {insert full birth name}, call to me the infinite resource of all that I am under **Universal Law**; and I now give intent that I remember and reclaim the sovereignty and integrity of my being and bodies as a Divine expression of **Universal Consciousness**. I call upon the **Essence of my Presence**, **my Guides** and **the Intelligence of Spirit** at the **Highest Level of the Light** to support and facilitate this process in me ... and I give thanks that this is so.
>
> Spirit, please work with me at every level: physical, emotional, mental and spiritual, and assist me to transmute and release the influence of any old fear-based programming that I carry and which prevents me from embodying and expressing the truth of my being.
>
> I invite any being or consciousness of the Light, who has experience and expertise in the areas relevant to me, to be with me, working through me, bringing guidance, direction and support. And I particularly ask the Consciousness of ... [insert the name of any guide(s) who you relate to strongly] for assistance with this.
>
> And throughout this process I ask that the space I occupy, this room, be completely filled and surrounded with Divine Love, Divine Light, Divine Truth and Divine Wisdom.

Setting my intent like this creates an altered space where it is safe for deep issues to surface. I can then enter into further dialogue (spoken aloud) to transform and release the tension and trauma underneath these issues. Often feelings will arise that were buried at the time of a particular incident in the interest of getting on with my life. It takes energy to keep these buried, energy that is more profitably used in living life. Also, whilst they are buried they can always be triggered even though I may have come to terms with an event intellectually. More will be said about this later, but for now remember that in the altered space of this process what you feel is what's leaving.

4.

The Gift of Sensitivity

*I just realized that there's going to be
a lot of painful times in life, so I better
learn to deal with it the right way.*

TREY PARKER AND MATT STONE
(SOUTH PARK, RAISINS, 2003)

FEELING AND SENSITIVITY

Sensitivity is basically our capacity for feeling. All of our sensitivity relates to our feeling capability, and it's our feeling capability that gives us access to our souls. The essence of who we are is our presence to our feelings. This is the core of the *principle of presence*. Our feelings tell us what is going on in the energy field – the field of *Universal Consciousness*. This is how we interface with spirit. We read energy through our feelings, spirit communicates to us through our feelings. Feelings cannot lie, but we can lie about them.

One of the main challenges facing us all is our insensitivity to our sensitivity. Few of us have any real appreciation of just how sensitive we are to the energies around us, and even less about how to be with or manage that sensitivity. This leads to a great deal of general insensitivity in every day life. In more mundane terms most people recognize their susceptibility to atmospheres, but fail to make the connection between their sensitivity and the energy of the *Field* because this is barely known about. However, these two phenomena are essentially the same thing.

> *Insensitivity to others demonstrates a basic*
> *insensitivity to oneself.*

Every one of us is an extremely sensitive being. But, because of the conventions of the consensus reality and the limitations of what might be called our mortal mind, any attribute of sensitivity is far more likely to be regarded as a curse than a blessing. Consequently the more sensitive we are, the more we have learned to conceal the fact, often resorting to defensive behavior patterns that ensure other human beings give us a wide berth. Some of the defense strategies employed can be offensive, some can be abusive, some can be violent and aggressive. They all come from fear and pain: the fear that our sensitivity will be exposed, exploited and ridiculed, and the pain of having experienced this treatment at the hands of others.

As babies, when we first enter this earth reality we are totally present to our feeling selves. We are wide open, and we feel *everything* going on around us. This openness tends to diminish as we go through life. We learn to shut down to our feelings. It is just too strenuous to feel everything and learn how to function in a physical body at the same time. Not only that, but feelings have no currency here for communication, so most of what we feel is the pain. This pain is not so much physical as the collective distress and anguish of all the other souls incarnated here, who are also grappling with the suppression of their sensitivity.

Have you ever wondered why it feels so good to get away from the city and escape to the mountains, the forest or the sea? What do you think you're escaping from? It might seem to be the pollution or the pressures of a busy life, but underneath it is the nourishing connection with the authenticity of nature that is so attractive. To be in a place where there is no artifice brings us into a healthier connection with the soul. This provides an invaluable respite from the background tension of pain and confusion in the environment.

That is why spending time outside the country where we were born and grew up can feel very expansive. When we are abroad we are free of the background control matrix that we have been subjected to on a daily basis from conception. Some personal exploits away from home can be quite outrageously abandoned for the same reason: at last people feel as if they can be themselves with nobody watching them to see what they are up to. Curiously when people return from living abroad for a prolonged period they can experience a kind of re-entry trauma as the old control matrix of the cultural collective closes around them again. Could there be a message here (from *Spiritual Intelligence*)?

We all contribute to the background matrix of our environment. Each one of us broadcasts our own energy signature, which is loaded with our beliefs, our values and our trauma. The cumulative sum of this in large centers of population is very intense and oppressive, which is why we need to get away from time to time. It is an artificial environment that demands artificiality from everyone living within its protection.

> *Sensitivity is the capacity to feel.*
> *Feelings are signals from the **Field** as it in-forms us.*

COLLECTIVE PAIN

The collective sum of the pain of every individual fills the space around us. It is constantly being broadcast into the energy field of where we live. This is the case whether we live in a peaceful environment or a violent one, simply because unless we have learned to be present with our sensitivity we have traumatized ourselves by suppressing it. This suppression creates an unconscious wound that festers away underneath the veneer of social competence that we develop in order to fit in with our respective social order. Everyone carries these unconscious wounds and contributes the effects to the collective.

It's worth saying here that the edict of the social order is the combination of the imperatives, norms, ideals, expectations, taboos, codes of behavior and values that we have to comply with in order to be accepted as a member of society. Another way of expressing this would be to call it our cultural programming.

It took me a while to learn the difference between what I felt from the collective, and what I felt as my own personal contribution. I'd been told what I should feel in particular circumstances, and required to demonstrate particular emotions to satisfy others' expectation. Somehow I was never able to reconcile this with what was really going on inside me, on some occasions noticeably so provoking heavy blame and criticism. It wasn't until I began to reclaim my own power and tell myself that whatever I felt was ok – even if other people didn't like it – that I began to be able to discern the difference between the collective energy and my own. For most people the inability to make this distinction is the norm rather than the exception, the majority being largely unaware that there is a difference. The interesting thing is that we all feel the collective in some way, and very few of us stop to consider exactly what it is we are experiencing. I encourage you to take a little time now to ponder the following questions. They will give you an indication of your sensitivity.

- When you wander into a strange part of town, can you tell whether it is friendly or not?
- Do you know when people have been having an emotionally charged argument, without having been present during the interaction?
- When you're in the company of someone you know, can you tell if they are depressed?
- Do you get a sense of expansion when you get away from the city into an area of nature?

- Are you able to tell when you are being heard, rather than listened to politely?
- Do you know when you are being followed?
- Do you feel crowded when someone stands too close to you during a conversation?
- Can you tell when someone is angry, without being told?
- Do you ever have a sense of knowing something is right for you – and override this with your mind to your regret?
- If you are around people who are excited, do you get excited?
- Do you know when you are being stared at?
- If you are around people who are miserable do you get miserable?
- Can you tell when others are pleased – or displeased – with you?

A 'yes' answer to any of these questions is an indicator that your sensitivity is operating effectively, and that you are picking up the *Field* loud and clear. If you were unable to give a yes response to any of them, the chances are you have shut down your sensitivity to a very painful extent. You may want to think about whether you want to continue in this condition. Either way the next question to ask yourself is, *Do I know how this is affecting me?*

> When Tom first came to see me he had just taken a new job on a busy trading desk at a high-profile investment bank. The new job was a big step up the career ladder and although Tom was very bright and well-qualified it was a bit of a stretch for him. But, worse than this, after only a month he felt he was failing. He dreaded his daily train journey into the office and was having nightmares.
>
> Tom had landed himself in an extremely pressurized working environment, where the stakes were very high. It had been the high stakes that had attracted him, as he found that aspect of the work exciting, but the other side of that coin was that any mistakes made took on a heightened significance. They were definitely noticed, and drew frowns from every quarter. Tom was afraid to venture any suggestions; he was afraid to take any initiative; he

was afraid to leave his desk before ten in the evening; he was afraid he wasn't working hard enough; he was afraid of being fired. The truth of his situation was that he was facing a major career and personal setback if he could not find his way through this jungle of fear. His job was destroying him.

What Tom had failed to take account of was his own sensitivity. He knew he was sensitive all right – he cried at sad movies, and was kind to his mother – but he did not realize he was sensitive to everyone in general. He hadn't considered that everyone in his office might be suffering similar anxieties to himself. He hadn't seen that the environment he worked in was not merely in-formed but structured by the fears he was feeling.

Everyone in the office was terrified that their own inadequacies would suddenly surface and cause their downfall and ruin for their trading group. And the major defense strategy against this was the widespread practice of blame and criticism. All of this was being broadcast at high intensity into the office ambience. Being sensitive Tom had picked this up without knowing. He was anxious enough about his own performance in a new job, but felt the endemic fear and tension of his office culture as well and thought it was all his!

When he learned to be present with his own sensitivity he was able to see how the others in his office environment might also be grappling with their sensitivity. They were all in a similar situation to him. It was just that some of his colleagues were more experienced at coping with it or hiding it than he was. No-one knew how to be with it, embrace it and use it. This realization was an epiphany for him.

He began to be sensitive to himself. When he felt his fear surfacing he stopped criticizing himself and started to be kind to himself. He told himself it was a tough environment and it was ok to be scared. Then he started to see his colleagues with compassion for their predicament. He began being kind to them. Inside a few months Tom became the most respected member of his team. He loved his job and was earmarked for promotion.

The fact is that the collective field does affect us all. It is a section of the *Universal Field* that has been conditioned by every member of a collective. As such it is an intelligence that subtly informs all of our actions with a sense of appropriateness – or otherwise – that we take for granted until we begin to see it and feel it. Whilst we hold a viewpoint that there is nothing to notice, we will notice nothing. Once we open up to the possibility that there maybe something going on that we've been unaware of, the effects of the collective field become more noticeable. It is then that we are at the point of a paradigm shift.

> ⮞ The next time you find yourself suffering in an environment, feeling weighed down, depressed, angry, stressed out, frustrated or afraid try an experiment. Simply find a way of extricating yourself. Take a little walk or go to the bathroom. Do something to physically remove yourself from the situation, and while you are removed notice how you feel. Then go back to the situation and see how you feel again. If there is any difference notice it. If you carry the heaviness or stress with you it is yours, but if you notice a sense of relief when you move away from the situation the chances are that the collective field is causing the discomfort – which means it is not all you.

If you find that you are susceptible to your environment in this way, you have learned at least two things. The first is that you are sensitive; the second that the collective field affects you. As you develop a spiritually intelligent way of being the effects will become less and your sensitivity will develop into discernment. The key to this is to be more present with yourself. The centering exercise given at the end of chapter one is one of the best tools for bringing you to presence. Use it whenever and wherever you find yourself caught up in the collective field, it will help you to stay open and witness your situation, rather than react or shut yourself down.

GENTLENESS

The range of our sensitivity, and the apparent handicap it confers on us, are issues we like to keep hidden. Most situations in everyday life demand that we ignore our feelings and get on with business. The message from society is that feelings are at best inconvenient, and at worst a good cause for rejection. Feelings are seen as aspect of existence that is an unwelcome intrusion into the smooth running of day-to-day business. So the imperative is to keep our feelings under control if we want to be accepted in the community at large. And it's very interesting that the way we know this is from *feeling* it in the collective mind-set.

So we are caught in a double bind. The key to freeing ourselves from the tyranny of the cultural collective is to allow ourselves to feel whatever is there and be present with our feelings. But cultural imperatives demand that feelings be suppressed and sanitized. That is, we are constrained to hold back our inner truth in order to have some measure of acceptance in our world. If we fail to comply we are likely to experience some form of rejection, a condition loaded with fear. In order to avoid this we inflict the suppression demanded by the social order upon ourselves. We rationalize this as self-discipline, but it is more accurately self-violation.

The fact is many of our cultural institutions are founded on self-violation in this way, through the *principle of approval*. We are accepted on pain of compliance with a particular code of behavior. Deep in our unconscious we know this, which is why many of us react so strongly to injustice. We're really reacting to the injustice we practice on ourselves in order to fit in where we believe we must.

> *Self-suppression is an unconscious version of self-rejection.*
> *It feeds the disease of low self-esteem that pervades*
> *western cultures.*

This is an extremely deep wound, the origin of which goes back centuries. The *principle of reaction* tells us that our reactions are the sign of an emotional or psychological wound that has not been healed. Just as treating a physical wound roughly aggravates the injury and impairs the healing process, the same is true for our invisible wounds. They are not an indication of failure in any sense; they are a sign of the deep pain we still carry. They show us where we can focus our intent to begin unraveling our self-destructive programming. So what we really need to practice is gentleness with ourselves, particularly with our emotional reactions. This is where our sensitivity has to be applied first and foremost, with ourselves.

PSYCHIC PROTECTION

There are many psychic protection techniques that can be employed to reduce the amount of toxicity you take on from the collective field of your environment. They will all have a degree of effectiveness and provide relief. However you will only take on something from your environment, or from another person, if there is a hook in you to hang it on. Another way of saying this that you will only take something on if there is a part of you that resonates with the external source. This is implicit in the *principle of interconnection.*

So if you take something on from the people around you it's not their fault – nor is it yours. Neither is it because they are operating at a lower vibration of consciousness than you. It's because there's some part of you that is in resonance with what is around you – be it pain, judgment, criticism, depression, despair, anger, resentment or joy. (Let's not get carried away and think it's only the so-called negative qualities we're talking about.) If you take something on it's a sign that there's something in you that you need to be present with and feel. That's all!

Although it may seem that once you've discovered that your environment is the source of your discomfort the best thing to do is shut yourself off, or disconnect in some way, I advise you to resist this temptation. I also advise you to resist seeing anyone else's pain, misery, projection or denial as something you must protect yourself against. Psychic protection techniques will shield you from the general toxicity of the collective field, but they will also prevent you from using what you take on as a guide for your own healing and empowerment.

If you are insulated from the stimuli that show you where your reactive patterns come from, it will take longer for you to get clear of them. Worse, you can actually develop a false sense of having nothing to really work on in yourself. Your transformative growth will be substantially impaired. It is therefore a dangerous assumption to think that you are so sensitive you've just got to have some protection up or you couldn't function in the world as it is. Psychic protection readily becomes a palliative that prevents you from becoming as fully conscious as you can be – it numbs you out. This is a subtle device of what is sometimes called the spiritual ego – the ego that identifies itself as spiritual and therefore ok, unlike all those other egos that haven't got a clue about the trouble they're in and which you have to protect yourself from.

In this way psychic protection is a device of separation rather than connection, so it anchors you in the paradigm you want to shift out of. Although it is only available to you as a consequence of raising your spiritual awareness, dependence upon it keeps you in the dark. The same is true for many practices that are called meditation and which are used to escape from the problems of life. More will be said about this in a later chapter.

As you develop your *Spiritual Intelligence* the hooks that got you caught up in the drama of external situations are gradually dissolved in the process. What this means is that all psychic protection is ultimately redundant. The more in alignment with your soul you are, the less toxicity you will take on, and you will become more comfortable with your sensitivity in situations that would simply have terrified you at one time. Nevertheless whilst you build your strength in your own center some protection is not only useful but necessary. It's a bit like protecting a seedling from the frost to give it a chance to establish itself, once it's established it needs to be free to grow into its own magnificence or it will remain stunted by the constraints of its early protected setting. For this reason I'm going to give you two protection strategies that I've found useful. You'll find these in the practical section at the end of this chapter.

PSYCHIC ABILITIES AND SENSITIVITY

Psychic ability originates in the connection with universal mind. The stronger your connection the more psychic ability you will possess. This does not necessarily mean that the information you access, nor your interpretation of it will be accurate. Many factors interfere in this area and it is prudent to make yourself aware of their relevance to you, because increased psychic awareness is endemic to the process of opening up to *Spiritual Intelligence*. Psychic awareness is inherent in the *principle of interconnection* and it manifests in intuition. Indeed, it cannot be avoided.

The response of the community to psychics themselves, and psychic awareness in general, is somewhat mixed. It ranges from adulation and respect to fear and condemnation. Neither end of this spectrum is appropriate or valid.

The expansion of psychic ability is a natural consequence of raising your level of consciousness. As you evolve spiritually your psychic ability will inevitably increase. But just because this is happening is no reason to assume that you are spiritually evolved. Nor is it safe to assume you are spiritually evolved if you have natural psychic gifts. This is one of the greatest misconceptions of the New Age movement, and popular culture. It results in serious submissive tendencies on the part of those who consider themselves less evolved. By that I mean there is a major temptation for people to give their power away to anyone who claims to be psychic, or who demonstrates psychic abilities.

This is actually damaging to all concerned. The psychics are placed on a pedestal, which encourages them to neglect their own growth. Everyone else involved takes up a position where they are likely to give greater significance to the psychic's opinion than their own wisdom. The truth is that we all have incredible inherent psychic ability, by virtue of our *Spiritual Intelligence* and the connection to *Universal Consciousness*. We are, however, largely unaware of this. But almost everyone can tell some story of having a strong non-rational knowing about an event yet to unfold that turned out as they suspected.

Psychic powers are referred to in eastern spiritual traditions as the *siddhis*. They are recognized as paranormal, or magical powers, manifesting as a disciple evolves along the spiritual path to *enlightenment*. They include clairvoyance, levitation, astral traveling (consciously journeying out of the body), and manifestation (causing physical artifacts to materialize from nowhere). But they come with a spiritual health warning. The *siddhis* are an indication that the disciple has begun the journey, covered the first few miles of the road and reached a resting place. If the disciple rests too long it will become even more difficult to set out on the road again. The message is that over emphasis on psychic powers is a serious distraction from the real journey.

> *When you are firmly committed to your path*
> **Spiritual Intelligence** *will communicate whatever*
> *you need to be aware of, in the most appropriate*
> *way for you, in the moment.*

There is nothing special about becoming psychic. What happens within the natural process of spiritual evolution is that we become progressively more aware of our psychic sensitivities. And because we are all unique beings, this happens in a different way for every one of us. Our biggest challenge with this situation is learning to interpret the information that comes, and knowing how to express it if that becomes necessary. The qualities required for this are clarity and discernment. These qualities may well be inherent within us, but they are distorted by the consensus reality mental strategies we adopt to survive in our personal worldly environment.

In the area of interpretation one of the biggest difficulties to overcome is the interference of our own emotional issues. These prejudice every facet of our self-expression. This is true for everyone. It is why the interpretations given by different psychic readers vary so much. Moreover, all psychic readers provide a channel for information from *Universal Consciousness* to express, but the integrity of information channeled cannot always be relied on. Many of them understand this, but many do not, and the vast majority believe in what they are doing so they can seem very authoritative.

All psychic information is distilled from some subtle aspect of collective consciousness. It is just as possible for your own unconscious fears to be channeled, or for the general fear-based consciousness of any particular interest group to be channeled, as it is for the higher wisdom of your eternal soul, or for any other level of consciousness. It is your responsibility to exercise discernment.

> *Everything anyone tells you will always be colored*
> *by the particular worldview they hold.*

What cannot be emphasized enough is that all the information that comes through psychic channels comes from the *Universal Field of Consciousness,* which encompasses the energy of absolutely everything – everything that has happened and the potential of everything that can happen. This is because of the law of entropy; all information is ultimately energy. Energy cannot be destroyed, or created, only qualified. We are receiving information from this source unconsciously at all times, it's what we were hearing before we developed a competence with language and learned to shut out the 'unwanted' background noise.

As has been mentioned before, we are also contributors to the background noise; that is we are unconsciously broadcasting our consciousness perspective through our energy fields. This means it is in our power to change the consensus environment of where we live. You might consider also that if we don't contribute to the change we contribute to a status quo. Once you know this it's easy to get off on a guilt trip about how you could be doing, or could have done more, but all that does is broadcast guilt, judgment and frustration into the collective – it makes it easier for others to feel guilty, critical and frustrated! Think about what it's like to be around someone who is continually depressed and gloomy, what it's like to be around someone who is enjoying the adventure of life with all its ups and downs. I encourage you to make it your intent to be the latter. The level of consciousness we hold, and aspire to is vitally important not only to ourselves but to the global collective.

One final point on this topic. When the connection with

universal mind is left more functional at birth, as it is with some people, it often makes for dysfunction in everyday life. The degree to which this connection is functional varies considerably, extreme cases are treated as mental illness and some of these individuals can be dangerously disturbed. Many of those whose cosmic memories have not shut down fully become what society recognizes as psychic, and it's interesting to note that most of these have great difficulty being grounded and present in the world. Everyday life often defeats them as they are distracted by their inner voices, or the visions and overwhelming feelings they are beset with. It can take an entire lifetime to master such a gift.

THE MYTH OF OBJECTIVITY

The existence of the *Field* and *Spiritual Intelligence* is a huge challenge to the conventions of objectivity, and what is real. I believe this is the main reason why these themes have remained outside mainstream thought and have been relegated to the realms of mysticism, esoteric practice and nonsense, even though the evidence for their veracity is mounting.

Objectivity is a curious concept. It is what theorists call a construct by which it is meant that it is artificial. However in this it is an unconscious construct, as it appears to arise as a natural truth. Objectivity rests in the assumption that all phenomena can be observed from a detached perspective, and this would seem to be the case. However, over the last century, the field of quantum physics has provided proof that the observer has a measurable effect on what is observed.

In the 1930s Wolfgang Pauli's collaboration with Jung[d] clearly indicated that the subjective was all there was for anyone to go on. Forty years on Fritjof Capra[e] was telling us that whereas in the old paradigm scientific descriptions were believed to be objective, in the new paradigm epistemology (how we know what we call knowledge itself) has to be included explicitly in the description of natural phenomena. That is to say it is now known that the concept of objective observation is fallacious. Yet there is an insistent demand for this objectivity everywhere in our culture.

In what we call everyday reality the effect of the observer may seem negligible, but it is there nonetheless. And if it is there the possibility exists that we can become more conscious of it, and maybe able to utilize it fruitfully.

There is another problem with objectivity in that the observer is a consciousness – a self-aware being – but the seat (or locus) and substance of that consciousness are yet to be defined. This means that the agency attempting to determine the objective reality of an observation is itself abstract and ineffable. Furthermore every human observation is filtered through the interpretive apparatus of this agency – the observer. And this apparatus is conditioned by everything that has contributed to the existence of the observer in his or her present form. This means that the observer is not an objective item, and it begs the question as to whether any observation made by such an observer could be objective.

It is, of course, very practical to have a convention of objectivity, but it is important to acknowledge that that is what it is: a convention. What happens with this convention, like every other, is that it gets subsumed into the unconscious and becomes a tenet of our self-identity. Remember the *principle of self-identity* tells us that self-identity itself is another construct of the mortal mind, one by means of which the mind basically signifies its own existence to itself. Thus we can expect strong emotional reactions to be triggered when the convention of objectivity is disputed.

Although they may not describe it like this, it is the absolute certainty that the concept of objectivity is a myth that enables skilled martial artists to punch through piles of bricks, and for yogis to demonstrate paranormal powers. Discipline and dedication have made it possible for these individuals to detach sufficiently from the collective consensus so that they are unbound by conventional reality. They are informed by *Spiritual Intelligence*; they inherently utilize the *principle of interconnection*; they take responsibility for their interpretation of reality and express their mastery accordingly.

All I have to go on in determining what constitutes objective reality for me is my own experience. This includes my experience of other people's description and interpretation of their experience. So I am totally responsible for what I consider to be objective reality. Ultimately this is all a matter of my own subjective interpretation, the interpretation produced by the consciousness that operates through me. This is a very great responsibility, and most people shy away from it, but it is a major principle of self-empowerment as outlined in chapter one – *the principle of self-identity*.

> *The myth of objectivity sabotages* **Spiritual Intelligence**.
> *It precludes the principle of interconnection and*
> *underwrites the illusion of separation.*

I can only determine what is true and relevant for me myself. No-one else is capable or competent to do this for me. In order to do this I have to trust myself unconditionally and make all of my decisions consciously. If I make a mistake, it may be an unpleasant experience, but I will have made it by my own conscious choice with a commitment to live with the consequences. I cannot be a victim when I operate like this. This is how my power is manifest, through the *principle of presence*.

A useful exercise to talk yourself through when determining what is true for you in the light of what you are being told goes like this:

> ➤ Is it true that this person/some people/many people think like this and believe in it?
> How much is my informant invested in what is being shared?
> Does it feel as if it nourishes and supports me?
> Does it undermine me, or anyone else?
> Is this what I want to adopt for myself?

This acknowledges that what you are hearing is true for some people, and at the same time leaves the door open for you to make your own decision about it. You are looking for a *yes* answer to the first question; and a *no* answer to the third to guide you towards your own truth. The second, fourth and fifth questions will lead you into taking responsibility for yourself.

It is not the job of this book to give you the techniques by which you can exhibit your mastery, but rather to assist you to open up to the possibility that your mastery can be demonstrated to you and that you can choose to live from that place. Developing *Spiritual Intelligence* is about developing an openness of perspective that the *Essence of your Presence* can express through and so do its work. That work will always challenge you to evolve beyond the limitations of what you think you know, to shift into a new way of being. Consciously choosing to embrace your sensitivity enables you to discern your potential and move towards it. Your sensitivity is your guide.

PRACTICAL

Psychic Protection

The best psychic protection of all is to follow the wisdom of your heart. Your heart will never let you walk into a situation that is a threat to your wellbeing. Basically if your heart says no, don't do it! However, as I promised I've included two strategies for psychic protection. One is a simple insulating or shutting out process, the other is much more flexible. The first procedure is as follows:

> ⮞ Imagine that you are putting on a huge dressing gown, one that reaches down to the floor and has a zip-up front. Before you go into a situation that you know is going to be difficult for you to cope with because of your sensitivity, physically go through the motions of putting this garment on. Zip yourself into it and for good measure tie the belt around your waist to keep it fastened. It's really effective to go through the motions of this with your body, as this is a focus for your intent. And your intent must be **I remain clear and centered at all times, in all situations.**

It is absolutely imperative that you make no statements like *I don't take anything on*, or *Other people's energies cannot attach to me*. These will have the opposite effect to the one you want.

The second strategy is to use an augmented form of the centering process I gave in chapter one. There is a little more visualization to go with this.

> ➤ Begin by bringing your energy field in as detailed earlier. Then imagine that somewhere way above your head is a source of light like the Sun but which is actually at the center of the cosmos. It is the grand central Sun of all existence, if you like. Next imagine a ray of light reaching out from this sun to the top of your head in the center, and penetrating to your heart. At the same time imagine another source of light below you at the center of the earth, and see this reaching up through your spine to meet the other ray in the center of your heart. Take a few breaths to establish this and envision that this light fills your heart to overflowing. Just before it overflows blow your breath out as if you are blowing a feather off the end of your nose, and imagine that the light from your heart suddenly expands into a sphere that encompasses your entire physical body. Say to yourself (or aloud if you can as that is better still): **I direct this light to hold me in a protected space safe, clear and centered in this < ... specific description of your needs ... > situation.**

With this procedure you are actually working with your energy field, and your intent. You can set it up with the intent for it to sustain itself with diminishing power as you develop your own strength, and you can set it to last for as long as you need it asking your soul (the *essence of your presence*) to control it for you. With this procedure you are claiming your right to be consciously in control of yourself.

Re-activation of Sensitivity
Working with intent and *Spiritual Intelligence* it's possible to revive and re-activate your sensitivity, when you're ready. It's important

that you only do this when you are ready as to do it too soon can cause you to shut down even further. The thing to watch for in yourself is if there's any judgment or criticism in you for having shut yourself down in any way. If there is, or any guilt or shame around the damage you might have created in yourself over the years by suppressing yourself, then take a step back and relax. You must realize that you have done your best with the information you had available, the facilities at your disposal and the circumstances you were living in. This has always been the case, even when you think you failed.

All of your life up to this moment – your experiences, your responses, your reactions – has brought you to this point where you are ready to look inside and deal with what you find there. Everything has been part of your learning, and has value. Even if you can't see this now, it will become clearer the more you engage with your personal growth. So don't rush into any of the processes given in this book (or elsewhere) out of a sense of guilt or shame, or with any belief that you wasted so much time before you began to wake up to yourself that you have a duty to catch up. This is just more self-criticism, and if it won't go away that's the place to start. Just sit with it and be present. Don't try to stop it, let it rant. At some point it will run out of steam. Understand that any voice of disapproval, wherever it comes from, is the voice of sabotage. It is siphoning off your attention and your energy and distracting you from your purpose so it's adding to the delay in engaging with your personal evolution.

As I've indicated before, it is advisable to create a sacred space for this ceremony, and to give yourself sufficient privacy to stay with any feelings that arise. When they do acknowledge them internally and breathe into them. Watch for any tightening in your body, especially your jaw, your chest, your shoulders, your spine or your solar-plexus. Deliberately relax and take your breath into the tension. When you are ready, give your intent by saying the following words aloud.

> ≈ Spirit, it's possible that I have suppressed my sensitivity in order to comply with the rules of my family, my relationships

and my culture. If this is true in any way, please go deep into my cellular memory – work with my mind and mental body, and my emotional body – and completely dismantle and release all the control strategies and devices I carry that prevent my sensitivity from being available to me, or from showing itself in the world at large. Melt away all the tension and trauma ever created in me as a consequence of the suppression of my sensitivity. Release and transform all the fear and terror of rejection, and all the shame and guilt engendered through cultural conditioning. Replace everything with Divine Love, Divine Truth and Divine Wisdom. Work holographically, throughout all lifetimes, all realities, all dimensions and all forms of existence, so that this is effective now in every aspect of my being across space and time and throughout the Universal Field of Consciousness. And I give thanks that this is so.

Once you've done this let go. You may find an instant response from *Spirit*; you may feel physical shifts inside your body; you may feel nothing. Things will change in time, and it may also take you some time to learn to notice them.

5.

The Soul Wound

*It all depends on how we look at things,
and not on how they are themselves.*

CARL JUNG

What I call the *Soul Wound* is the root of all the pain and despair in the world, and it's an illusion. This chapter will offer an explanation of how that illusion is structured, and how we sustain it. This is intended to give your mind something to reflect upon, rather than lay down an absolute definitive form. The form is not the issue, neither is the reason or content. This is where we all get stuck if we look for these alone. The main purpose is to examine the dynamics of how we create our illusions and compound them into monsters that we are then terrified to confront.

THE TRAUMA OF INCARNATION

These days, the trauma of birth is well recognized as having a huge affect on our development as personalities. It is still overlooked by the bulk of humanity when they consider why they are like they are in life. So it's worth going over the salient points here.

For the time being we'll ignore any *in utero* stresses experienced by the fetus and consider the ideal. In the womb the fetus is completely supported. It is warm, maintained at body temperature. It is insulated from noise. It is in complete darkness, and it is supplied with oxygen via the amniotic fluid inside the placenta. Contrast this with the conditions existing outside the womb and there is only one word to describe the experience of the transition from one to the other – shock.

In the modern way that birth occurs in western civilizations the fetus is pushed and pulled into an atmosphere that is likely to be a full ten degrees Celsius below the temperature of its uterine environment. The abrupt cooling effect on the skin is aggravated by the evaporation of any fluid on its surface. The ears have, up until this moment, been insulated from all of the harsh sounds of the world. All of a sudden there is an explosion of disconnected noise as the child enters the excitement of the delivery room. The eyes, that have never yet seen any light whatsoever, are suddenly exposed to the intensity of the birth environment. In a modern hospital the lighting level will be very bright. Lungs that have never drawn breath are suddenly inflated with relatively cold air that strikes with rasping pain. This assault on the senses completely overwhelms any other feelings or sensations.

All of this is relevant enough in itself, but there is much more. The fetus has already had physical existence as a part of the mother's body and has been *in*-formed by this. We felt her pain, her fear, her tensions and anxieties, even the residue of her unresolved birth trauma. We felt all of this as indistinguishable from our own, without being able to make sense of any of it. So in addition to the physical shock there is an inherent confusion engendered by any tension our mother felt, and any anxieties she carried. This is what happens in a relatively good situation, and it would seem to be enough to cope with but if there are complications of any kind they will aggravate the confusion.

This is how most of us begin life on earth. Virtually everything of a subtle nature is blotted out by the barrage of information bombarding our physical senses. You can begin to understand a lot about yourself, and others, by considering who has to make some kind of sense out of all this chaos and what are the resources available for this task:

- What, or who, is the active intelligence engaged in establishing a physical existence?
- What are the terms of reference available?
- Where does the information come from?
- How can the information be classified and managed?
- Where do the classifying and management criteria originate?
- When did it all seem to start?

There is only one person involved in the making of sense – the newborn. There may be other people around, but initially none of the conventions of communication are in place. No-one understands the newborn and the newborn understands nothing. It cannot ask a question or be given an answer. Everything has to be self-generated.

It should be no surprise to realize that one of the first things we look for is the volume control to turn it all down a bit. The main difficulty that arises out of this is that we begin to regard our sensitivity as a handicap. We find ways to shut it down and ignore it; most of these originate from the mind, which creates all our emotional reactions based on the fear of feeling. This fear may ultimately trace itself back to the fear of feeling overwhelmed and totally disconnected. Whatever this process may be, when we shut our feelings down we close ourselves off to the greater part of who we are. We learn to manage our sensitivity by suppressing it (see the previous chapter). It is likely that this was a valid approach as we were growing up, but part of the spiritual journey is to open up to it and recognize it for the gift that it is.

A cardinal feature of the mortal mind is that under stress it goes into survival mode where it is polarized, operating only in terms of good and bad. Any experience of contrast or difference tends to be classified in these terms. This may be a functional requirement of the organism in relation to its environment, but it contributes greatly to the sense of fear and trauma at our birth. Moreover, such basic classifications persist long after they have any relevance to our situation.

Another factor that compounds the apparent chaotic nature of our birth experience is our lack of boundaries. As infants our sense of separation has yet to crystallize; we are unable to distinguish clearly any boundaries. We are wide open. We feel the background energy matrix of artificiality, and the pain of everyone struggling to fit themselves into the required patterns of behavior. We feel this pain and think that it must belong to us. In addition, because this pain appeared to originate with our arrival, we link the two together; we mentally associate. This association process is a function of how the mortal mind operates, and it supports a belief that we are responsible for all the pain.

Because we can't remember doing anything bad enough to have caused it all, we start to worry that we must be terrible in ourselves. This, of course, holds an inherent explanation of why we could have been rejected or abandoned, and it makes us particularly vulnerable to control through a sense of guilt and shame.

The effect of this state of affairs is that, in the physical realm, we tend to interpret our life experience as trauma virtually from the moment of conception. We set up beliefs about ourselves and our environment from a place of pain long before we have any understanding of our situation. These beliefs get buried in our unconscious and underwrite our core issues – the wounds, the suffering, the fears and the resentments that pattern our lives.

> Gillian was born during an air raid on London in World War II. Her mother was in the maternity section of a large hospital where she was relatively safe as expert medical attention was on hand. However, the delivery was about halfway through when the air-raid warning was sounded. This notched up the anxiety and tension levels considerably. Then the bombs started falling, and explosions could be heard in the surrounding area.
>
> Gillian was pushed and dragged into the world in an atmosphere of panic and terror. As soon as she was clear of her mother's body

the umbilical cord was cut. She was snatched away and bundled into a blanket. Then everyone was evacuated to the nearest air-raid shelter. But in the rush Gillian's head was bumped against the wall by the nurse carrying her. Fortunately there was no damage ... except ...

Sixty years later Gillian showed up for a consultation. She was finding it difficult to stand up for herself in her marriage and with her now grown-up children. She found it virtually impossible voice her true feelings for fear she would be overridden and shouted down.

In session she was feeling tension in her neck and head. After inviting *Spiritual Intelligence* to intervene and bring to her awareness what was underneath the tension Gillian recounted the dramatic story of her birth, which her mother had told her. She reported that they had often laughed at how clever and successful Gillian had become academically after her bang on the head. Gillian also began to remember how she had always had difficulty with being fully present with people. She literally thought that if she was noticed someone would pull her out of where she felt safe and try to kill her. Somewhere in Gillian's cellular memory all the details of her introduction to the world were still active.

At the level of her cellular memory Gillian saw the world as a place where she was constantly in danger of being seen, and snatched away from where she was safe. It was a perilous place that couldn't wait to inflict physical harm on her. Whereas the truth of her situation had been that there was a frantic effort to keep her secure and intact.

A major pattern that Gillian had developed was to hide herself away to the extent that she hid herself from herself. She could not allow herself to recognize any of her achievements in case she inadvertently drew attention to herself. So she never took on a leading role in any of the work she did. She allowed other people to take the recognition and the rewards for her efforts because she feared exposure of any kind. In spite of being highly intelligent and academically accomplished she felt inside that she was worthless and had nothing of value to share with people.

THE TRAUMA OF SEPARATION

The *perceived* trauma of separation is the *Soul Wound*, and I say *perceived* because this trauma is actually an illusion created through a limited interpretation of the mortal mind. The ambient condition that gives rise to the trauma of separation is the trauma of incarnation. In some ways the trauma of separation could be seen as a projection backwards in time from the trauma of incarnation, this arises from making a decision about the origin of an experience based on assumptions about its arrival. This is a virtual trauma, but it is nonetheless a construct that underpins our self-identity; one that validates itself in the way it continually seems to manifest in lived experience.

> *The illusion of physical existence is that we are on our own, separate and individual. Yet we carry the information within that this is a lie.*

The root of this separation 'trauma' lies in the *principle of interconnection* and its denial in the consensus reality. So let's look at how it works.

It is a condition of incarnation into a physical body that the mortal mind has to be tuned to function in a way that corresponds to the physical reality of the body. For the entity we know as the human being to coalesce into a coherent functioning unit, the non-physical has to be ignored, at least initially. A predisposition towards the non-physical realm makes no sense; it would constitute a distraction that jeopardizes physical survival. All our energy is required to focus on getting some degree of independent control over our bodies and establishing a healthy vehicle through which to express. Herein lies a seed of the separation that prejudices the physical world against the subtle or spiritual. The paradox is that the physical world could not exist without the spiritual, and is in fact comprised of the same substance anyway. This paradox is the fundamental concept embodied in the *principle of interconnection*.

The intensity of the physical human experience is so overpowering that it dominates everything else, so any notion of a connection with the greater reality and universal mind (*Universal Consciousness*) is completely displaced. In most of us the subtle realms are so completely blotted out that we become unaware of their existence.

Most people are given reminders of another kind of reality through what we might term uncanny experiences. These will include coincidences, premonitions and intuitions of all kinds but we are conditioned to disregard these through the *principle of approval* and the instrument of its enforcement – humiliation. There has been no room for the subtle in the modern social order. What supports our social conventions is approved of; whatever calls them into question is maligned. The "supernatural" has no place in the rational world of scientific materialism, so it is sanitized by religion where it is made safe by prescribing the conditions governing any engagement with it.

The effect of this is that our multidimensional and universal nature is obscured from us. What I mean by this is that our sense of self is limited to our self-identity and what is allowed by the conventions of our social order. We don't so much forget who we really are and where we come from as have the *in*-formation encoded within us, with no apparent access to the key. However because this is neither a complete disconnection, nor an obliteration, we are left with a haunting feeling that something is missing – something true and absolutely wonderful.

This feeling nags at us throughout our lives. It drives an incessant search for completeness, something to fill the emptiness. The feeling is made more profound by a vague memory that whatever it is was once a part of us. This is our inherent knowing that we are a part of the *Universal Field of Consciousness* that is ultimately all One.

The lingering feeling that something is missing maps directly onto the physical shock of birth. That part of us that supported and sustained us without any effort on our part – our mother – is suddenly gone. This is something that occurs before we are able to give any articulation to the experience. It's like we are set up to fall into a deep, deep, hole the top of which appears as a tiny pinpoint of light that is almost imperceptible in the distance.

What this engenders is a deep sense of separation – separation from the spiritual, separation from the source of our sustenance, separation from ourselves. This is a sense that we have been torn from whatever, or whoever, gave us the experience of being whole and complete. This is the trauma of separation. This trauma haunts every relationship ever entered into at the physical level of existence, because we are looking to replace what we have lost.

Furthermore the severity of the shock of our transition into the physical is such that we think something must have gone wrong. The consequences of this are that we make mortal mind (physical reality) interpretations of the circumstances we find ourselves in. Because we are scared and overwhelmed by our situation, and there is no reassurance that we are able to make sense of, the prevailing interpretation is of something having gone wrong. At this stage in our development we are still unlikely to have acquired any skill in the articulation of our feelings, and our minds will be polarized around what distresses us and what doesn't.

The truth is that nothing has gone wrong at all. It is absolutely vital that our mortal minds are tuned to our physical reality. Where this tuning is incomplete in any way it can result in serious mental dysfunction. Nevertheless, despite the crucial nature of this tuning, we *feel* the loss, and we *think* we are at fault. This forms a blueprint against which we will judge all our experiences from this point on. The principal core issues that develop out of all this are abandonment, rejection and worthlessness, and these sustain everything else.

THE ROOT OF EMOTIONAL REACTION

The engine of all this trauma is our sensitivity. There is something of a cosmic irony here as our sensitivity is exactly the evidence we've been looking for to confirm our connectedness. As has been detailed, we are all far more sensitive than has been realized or recognized. We feel the emotional resonances of the planet and all its inhabitants – some feel this more than others. Some don't know that they feel it. But what it means is, that more than anything else, we need to develop clarity and discernment to allow us to separate our reactions from those of others around us. Our job is only to clean up our own reactive patterns; it is not possible to clean up anyone else's and it can be a major distraction to try.

> *Your sensitivity is the clearest sign that you are*
> *still connected to your source.*

When you came into this world you were thrust into a complex web of chaos and confusion, where nothing made sense. It was your job to learn how to survive here through whatever means were at your disposal. You had to learn how to interpret your surroundings, and yourself, and the main instrument for this was your mortal mind.

In order to survive here it is essential that the mind is aligned with physical reality, but this has complications due to the self-reflexive nature of the mortal mind, which supports the paradigm of separation. However, it is the inherent function of the *Field* to manifest the *principle of interconnection*. This means that there is only one paradigm for existence – the paradigm of connection. Yet by some curious inversion almost our entire understanding of human existence is based on the paradigm of separation as perceived and nourished by the mortal mind. This is the essential existential paradox that we embody.

> *The alignment of the mortal mind with the*
> *physical reality it inhabits ensures that it is*
> *misaligned with* **Universal Mind**

Before you acquired language the mind had no coherent means of articulation so it processed your feelings. Broadly speaking this would have happened in the context of distress and delight, what felt agreeable and what felt disagreeable. The pre-linguistic conclusions it came to were somehow filed away in a manner that remains inaccessible linguistically, but which can nevertheless still be triggered. This can happen whenever the unconscious registers something that has been associated with those early feelings.

Your mind is an incredible tool. It registers every experience you have, and it files the information associatively. This does not follow a linear logic. So you can be surprised by thoughts of seemingly unrelated incidents that have a long forgotten common associative element. The irrationality of this when it occurs can leave you wondering. This irrational association has become a stereotypical tool of psychologists and psychoanalysts in looking for the underlying causes of behavioral discrepancies.

Also the mind is really good at creating structures, creating mental models that represent you to yourself in direct relation to your surroundings; this process manifests in the *principle of self-identity*. Having been inundated with intense experiences and strange energies the mind sets about making some kind of sense out of the total nonsense it perceived. It does this through an endless process of contrast, differentiation, association and deduction. If you consider that the only datum point it has is the seeming anarchy of the birth process you'll see what an incredible job it does, but it is the lack of a reliable datum that is problematic. The solution of the mortal mind is brilliant; it uses itself as its own datum. Unfortunately because of its misalignment in relation to *Universal Mind* from this point on the mortal mind is doomed to continually create inversions of the truth – inversions that become its deepest values and beliefs.

Once the mind has created a structure that seems to work it moves on, building upon the structure it has made time and time again, following the pattern of its original apparent success. The original structure, which was really only a premise with no objective foundation, becomes the starting point for your concept of reality and your beliefs about yourself.

Before too long the original structure is buried under a complexity of thought forms and strategies, and forgotten. Well it's not really forgotten; it transforms into a sub-routine and passes out of conscious awareness leaving you with beliefs and values that feel as if they are the core truth of your being. The only truth being that these beliefs have become associated with your early survival modes and instincts, without any real foundation. It will feel terrifying if they are challenged in any way, because this challenges the mental structure that represents your entire existence to yourself, without you being aware that this is happening. Any such challenge is likely to produce a strong emotional reaction, because it effectively threatens your existence.

Nothing of the sort is actually happening, but the deepest of our core issues take life in this way. They play out in everyday situations that are often trivial in themselves, but which somehow reflect those earlier traumatic experiences that the mortal mind subsumed into its construct of identity. Holding on to all of this consumes a tremendous amount of your life-force energy

THE BASIC CORE SEPARATION ISSUES

What follows is a hypothesis for the processes by which our core separation issues come into being. It is not meant to be a rigorous scientific exposition. At the moment there is no science that can verify these formulations; they are essentially subjective observations that emerge out of the mental differentiation of two perceived (felt) states of existence: that of feeling fully connected to *Universal Consciousness* and *Spiritual Intelligence*; and that of feeling completely disconnected. This is a bi-polar logic grounded in feelings; it can be reduced intellectually to the polarized concepts of PRESENCE and ABSENCE, but that is still only a representation of the process not the process itself.

The mortal mind builds interpretations of the sensual input it receives from the body through contrast and differentiation. The interpretations are generic rather than specific; they nevertheless founder on the inherent characteristic of the mind that causes its interpretations to tend towards an inversion of the truth. Because of the lack of a clear datum, the mortal mind is unaware of this, and every time its polarized interpretation is replicated with apparent success any falsehood becomes deeper ingrained. Our core separation issues cannot be anything other than fabrications, but they are locked in through physical sensual input. This is exactly how anchoring techniques are used in hypnotherapy. So perhaps there's a chance that we can recalibrate the mind and free ourselves from the tyranny of our core separation issues.

There is really only one primary core issue – separation from spirit, but this manifests in three main variations: abandonment, rejection and worthlessness as outlined generically below.

Abandonment: You are suddenly aware of a feeling in space and time. This feeling is new; it may be the first feeling you experience in the physical realm and it begs the question of what was there before it started. That means that what was there before must be gone, because what is there now is new. What is there now is a background matrix of pain, tension and anxiety. It is not integrated. If this is different from what was there before it perhaps what was there before was integrated.

Having felt that you were at some point fully integrated and supported in your existence, by an all-encompassing source (*Universal Consciousness*), this is contrasted with the new feeling. It may be that being fully integrated with the *Field* was no feeling, but the new *dis*-integrated feeling supersedes whatever was there before, so it feels as if all support has been withdrawn. You come to the conclusion that you have been left – abandoned in a hostile environment – to survive by your own devices. You know *Spirit* is there but you can't feel the connection.

To you this feels as if the connection has been severed. And it must be that *Spirit* has severed the connection, because you know you would never have done it – it was too precious to you.

Holding the belief that you've been cut off is too painful to endure. To alleviate the pain a decision is made to stop looking for the support that once must have been there, because it's gone, never to return. Its absence feels so total that it's as if it was never there in the first place. In any case it would be sheer cruelty to have treated you in this way; how could you possibly align yourself with an intelligence that could be so viciously and callously cruel? Right here is where *you* abandon *Spirit*; and this is the inversion because you abandon sprit but think it's the other way around!

All of this engenders a deep sense of betrayal leading to resentment, bitterness, jealousy, neediness and victimhood. It becomes the truth of your reality and constitutes a generative pattern that will seek corroboration in every aspect of your life

Rejection: You know you have always been an integral part of the wonder of all there is (*Universal Consciousness*). This knowledge is inherent in the *in*-formation that resides in your molecular and cellular structure. It just is. Suddenly you find yourself in a position where you feel a difference; this can only mean you are no longer an integrated part of the whole. All you can feel is the background matrix of tension, anxiety and pain of the earthly environment. This is terrifying.

What catastrophe could have caused this? You know *Spirit* is there but you can't feel the vital interconnectedness that you need to sustain you. You make an interpretation that what you feel is an indication that you have been cast out from where you were kept safe, nurtured and nourished – you feel rejected.

You would never have left voluntarily, so you must have been expelled and exiled to this dreadful place of chaos and lovelessness. The only explanations for this are either that you did something disastrously and unforgivably wrong; or that there is something inherently bad about you that has just come to light. Each of these conditions makes your continued acceptance impossible.

But how could an all-encompassing consciousness reject an integral part of itself unless it was diseased? How could there be so little compassion? How could you not be given an opportunity to redeem yourself and be reinstated? You couldn't possibly align yourself with any consciousness or intelligence that has so little compassion. Right here is the inversion where *you* reject *Spirit*, although you think it's the other way around. This engenders a deep sense of unworthiness, which leads to guilt, judgment and self-criticism. Just as in the previous model, it becomes the truth of your reality and constitutes a generative pattern that will seek corroboration in every aspect of your life.

Worthlessness: As an integral part of *Universal Consciousness*, you were complete. Completeness constituted your reality. Your presence as a part of the whole contributed to its completeness; its vastness was your vastness, its equilibrium yours. The universe was not complete without you. Suddenly you feel different. Your new feeling is *in*-formed by the pain, tension and anxiety of the background matrix. You no longer feel in balance, which translates into a loss of equilibrium.

Up to this point, absolutely everything you ever needed has always been available to you. You had everything; you were everything. Now you find yourself in a situation where you can no longer feel the presence of whatever it was that completed you – and what you made complete in itself.

This loss is devastating. How could your absence be missed? How could you have been lost? How could you have been allowed to disappear? If you were so precious, how could you not be missed? How could what was so precious to you have disappeared without warning? How are you going to exist without it? And if it can exist without you what does that signify about your value? You must be worthless! Not only that, it can't be worth trying to maintain a connection with any intelligence that doesn't miss you.

Maybe the contribution your existence made to the whole was not just negligible, but valued at absolute zero and therefore deserving of no support. But your conscious awareness knows that you do still exist; you are still something even though you don't know what that is.

Well ok, you decide that you will have to create your own support system. Its abundance will be used to sustain you alone. You will create your own completeness and refuse to share it with the universe, because it will be of no value to the universe anyway! Right here is the inversion where *you* lose *Spirit*, although your motivation comes from interpreting the situation as *Spirit* losing you.

This thought-form engenders a deep sense of isolation and dispossession, leading to resentment and bitterness, as well as voracious greed and the need to control and possess. Again, it will become the truth of your reality and constitutes a generative pattern that will seek corroboration in every aspect of your life.

These are the patterns of the three most basic thought-forms that create our core issues. Remember you have no words available to you when they are initiated. The words here are provided merely to demonstrate how the patterns can develop. There are other models that would work equally well, but to get stuck on the words is to miss the underlying energy of the process.

The core issues that are instituted by these thought-forms are haunted by the *principle of separation*; they broadly relate to the lower three chakras – root, sacral and solar plexus. These are the main energy centers that need to be cleared as we evolve our level of consciousness.

As individuals we all carry at least one of these issues predominantly, and the other two are generally present in a less prominent manner. But as each issue originates from the same basic situation one will translate or shape-shift into another if we chase them analytically. As we go through life any one of these may inform our thoughts and actions at any time, and we may cycle through all three.

It is worth noting that none of the core issues is at all easy to resolve. We have been working on them for a long long time, throughout our incarnational cycles. We know intrinsically through the *principle of in-formation and in-tuition* that there is no separation, no abandonment, no rejection. Yet even with the amount of practice afforded by several incarnations we still struggle, because the intensity of the feeling experience is so profound and the illusion of separation so strong.

The imprint of trauma created through the illusion of separation is resistant to any mental technique for overcoming it, because it was created by the mind as a self-defining parameter. What this means is that any challenge to it is regarded as a threat to the existence of the self-identified mortal mind, and this is translated into a threat to physical survival. This produces abject terror. So relying on mental processes to clear any of these patterns is a bit like agreeing with someone that one of you must die, handing them a loaded gun and expecting them to shoot themselves. Guess who gets shot! The achievement of any measure of imperviousness to this imprint is therefore a demonstration of the Mastery we are evolving to.

In the general consensus reality that we inhabit where our sensitivity is swamped by the mass and intensity of physical experience, the sources of our sufferings are so numerous that it's just not possible to identify them all. However, the processes by which we create and absorb them are few. Inviting *Spiritual Intelligence* to intervene in our own process helps us to hone our discernment so that we become more conscious of the effects of the collective. The more we can do this the more easily we are able to detach from situations that have no direct relevance to our own issues. This in turn helps us to register the insights that are relevant, and do something about them.

PRACTICAL

Before you attempt either of the procedures given in this section it is advisable to create a sacred space as described in chapter three. When you have done this, pay attention to any feeling sensations presenting in your body. It is quite likely that there will be a lot of fear. Whatever is there it is imperative that you allow it to be there. Do not try to push it away, pretend it isn't there or ignore it.

What you feel is what is leaving. Acknowledge it internally and breathe into it. By this I mean focus on your breath, and as you inhale direct your breath into the feeling with your mind. Stay with this until you feel yourself beginning to relax. Any time you notice your breathing tightening up, or getting shallow, deliberately relax your jaw and take a deep breath through your mouth.

The self-identity of the mortal mind is the biggest barrier to moving beyond the soul wound. It is such a deeply ingrained effect that it can only really be moved through with the assistance of the soul. This means you cannot decide intellectually when it is time for you to make the shift in consciousness that it brings. It is in effect a death and rebirth. It feels like a complete psychotic breakdown, which in some ways it is as the entire reality-base is being revised.

However having an intellectual understanding of the generic archetypal formation process will enable you to become more conscious of where you are operating through core issues. This prepares the mortal mind for the letting go process. The mind starts to see the necessity for it to allow itself to fall apart in order to be reconstituted in a way that promotes greater effectiveness and proficiency.

The first step is to invite *Spiritual Intelligence* to assist you to notice your soul wound programming, which you can do by saying the following words aloud:

> 〰 Spirit, please work with me on every level – physical, emotional, mental and spiritual. Connect with my inner guidance and increase my awareness of my soul wound. Help me to see all of the places this informs my thought processes and my actions, so that I can understand myself better and begin to make decisions that are more grounded in Universal Wisdom.

It's a good idea to begin a journal for this work. Keep a note of the insights you get and see if you notice any particular patterns emerging. In later chapters there will be some procedures for dealing with these secondary patterns. But for now just note them down, and do your best to stay present with them. By this I mean don't try to pretend to yourself that you haven't seen them – because they may not be very pretty. Accept them and remind yourself that it's ok to have these patterns; they are not you; they are what you have taken on. You have taken them on for one reason only – to discover them and clear them from your part of the collective consciousness. This is an act of compassion and service to all humanity. So any time you get into self-judgment with this self-exploration you slow the process and perpetuate the dysfunction.

The next step is to actually give intent to make the shift beyond the soul wound. Know that this will not happen instantly. It may be a number of years before you're ready to embody the changes it will bring, but *Spiritual Intelligence* will know the appropriate time for you. So when you feel ready, give your intent aloud as follows.

> ⮆ Spirit, it's possible that I carry a deep imprint of trauma that relates to the feelings of separation from Universal Consciousness I experienced when I came into the world. Please go deep into my cellular memory, work with my mind and mental body, and my emotional body, and completely melt away all the tension and trauma ever created in me as a consequence of the process of incarnation.
>
> Dismantle all the thought-forms and any mind-sets that cause me to think, feel, believe or behave as if I have been abandoned by Spirit, I have been rejected by Spirit or that I have lost my Spiritual connection. Bless my illusion with Love and realign it with Universal Wisdom.
>
> Wherever I have incorporated the illusion of the trauma of separation from Spirit into my self-identity, please erase all the mental and emotional triggers and the neuro-pathways that support or sustain this illusion within me. Do all of this in the optimum timing and manner for me and replace everything with Divine Love, Divine Truth and Divine Wisdom. Work holographically, throughout all lifetimes, all realities, all dimensions and all forms of existence, so that this is effective now in every aspect of my being across space and time and throughout the entire Akashic Field.
>
> I give thanks that this is so.

After you have uttered either of the above statements, give yourself some quiet time to feel the impact of your intent. Know that you do not have to know how anything is going to happen, but if you are sincere what you have given intent for will manifest.

6.
Projection – Friend and Enemy
A *good* teacher protects his pupils from his own influence.

BRUCE LEE

There are lots of good psychology textbooks that will detail the mechanism and theory of projection. However, what is needed for our purposes is a basic understanding of the process at an honest subjective human level and a spiritually intelligent perspective.

This chapter, at the center of the book, contains what is perhaps the most important deconstruction of our temporal way of life presented in these pages. The impact of the *principle of projection* is not easy to fully appreciate, but it is vital to gaining the insight needed to progress beyond the mundane and move into a more enlightened way of being. Perseverance with this material will pave the way to freeing your mind and to discovering and living what is true for you.

Projection is a term that comes from psychoanalysis. It is one that is gradually finding its way into general currency as the personal development movement grows to a wider acceptance. The *principle of projection* is one of the fundamental features of the human condition. Projection characterizes every aspect of our relationships – personal, collective and political; it is inextricably coupled with our self-identity; and it figures heavily in the emotional reactions set off by the mortal mind to conceal the artifice of its own construction. That is to say projection is a mental defense strategy, and although it may appear to keep us safe it is actually an act of disempowerment because it is an investment in our fears.

> *Projection is the device by means of which we give most of our power away.*

Projection describes the process whereby we see the images of our internal world as our external reality – if you think about the movie projector displaying images on a screen the metaphor is remarkably accurate. Projection is the agency by which we experience our internal process as external. The converse of this is that what we regard as external must always reflect back to us something relevant to our internal process.

In the context of personal development projection is frequently frowned upon, especially when we apply it to other people. To tell someone they are projecting is often used as a put-down. But the projection process goes on all the time, with everything in our world. So, rather than waste any energy trying to stop it, we might as well embrace it and see how holding a different level of consciousness around it can serve us.

Even in this world of personal development where teachers, therapists and facilitators are trained to see the issues of others with crystal clarity they fail to see their own, with various unconscious and disappointing consequences. The situation of the person in authority is a prime set up for people to give their power away – project it onto the expert. And the expert is supposed to get it right, so s/he is primed for denial to conceal anything that might be perceived as a shortcoming.

It is so EASY for teachers, therapists and facilitators to project their issues and agendas onto a client, a class or seminar group – and then proceed to fix the client/group rather than consider themselves as a possible source. This practice is endemic in the healing professions and it takes a lot of commitment and vigilance to get beyond it. The first step in cleaning this up is to acknowledge that it happens and that it will continue to happen. Stop trying to pretend it doesn't apply to me or you. It does, and it's ok.

The essential point to be clear on is that we all see the world as we think we are. My worldview is essentially a personal interpretation of myself and my relationship to my environment – my perceived world. This is inherent in the *principle of self-identity*, and we have no alternative but to begin our investigation from this place. This is quite a puzzle, because we have no objective references, so everything we conclude may be wrong. The possibility exists that nothing is as it seems; a possibility that is so terrifying that there is an almost automatic compulsion, an existential imperative, to deny it. This turns into a collective denial that can lead to suppression by the most violent means.

MAKING SENSE OF OURSELVES

One way to consider how projection functions is to see it as originating in the human ability to make mental models and structures, and to notice patterns that fit these structures. Initially this might begin in the noticing of a difference between two events or conditions. Then another difference is noted and the new *differential* conditions are associated with the original conditions or events. This happens *not* because any of the events or conditions displays a similarity, but simply because they are perceived through a similar dynamic process – differentiation.

The common associative element is the dynamic operation itself – the comparative lens of differentiation. At this point the actual difference is unimportant and may have no value, however this soon begins to change as conditions and events are related to feelings particularly the differential of pair anxiety and contentment. This is when preferences and prejudices are born.

Differentiation gives us the ability to make sense of ourselves to ourselves, and make sense of the world we live in. Making sense of things in this way is a generative and associative process. We gradually build up a context in which we position ourselves according to our interpretation of the circumstances of our lived experience. THIS IS NOT AN OBJECTIVE POSITION. Nor can it ever be, for anyone, yet it is how we live and share our existence with those around us.

In order for this to work it means that those around us MUST SHARE some of our interpretations of the general circumstances of existence. When we do find a shared interpretation we pretend to ourselves that we have found an objective truth, and the more people we can find to share the interpretation the more established the notion of objectivity becomes. This feeds a need for some sense of security, something intrinsically lacking as a consequence of the trauma of separation. What we are really doing is colluding with an external source to relieve the anxiety of our own sense of insecurity. WE ARE AVOIDING FEAR.

Our shared interpretations engender a social order and become adopted as truth. They nurture a culture of might is right, and can be traced in notions of majority rule. If everyone does it or accepts it then it must be ok. These shared interpretations then govern what is *right* and what is *wrong*. They are held in place by the fear of rejection and abandonment that lurks in the background, the consequence of the illusion of the trauma of separation that informs the mortal mind. Any dissent is in itself a separation that can trigger this fear – how difficult it is for any of us to go against the crowd. So the essential paradigm of our consensus reality is constituted in separation and fear, whatever other name it goes by.

This is a vast subject. If you think about the complex process of how we learn differentially through our sensory input, constantly testing and comparing, and the classification structures we are driven to adopt by the individuals involved in our upbringing (the social order), there's enough material to create a treatise. Really contemplating all of this can send the mind into a spiral of panic – a fear that we will want to suppress quickly. The required suppression is generally achieved through a process of prohibition: it is regarded as dangerous, stupid or even insane to go exploring this territory, so the door is closed by the simple expedient of making it wrong.

The other thing that can happen with the mind in this situation is that it can simply stop co-operating with the understanding process. When this happens it blanks itself off and induces a sense of tiredness. If any of this is happening to you at this point in your reading, know that you're on to something important to you and try the following exercise:

> ⚋ Raise your eyes from the page and allow yourself to gaze straight ahead. Move your eyes from left to right backwards and forwards three times. Then move them up and down three times. Then move your eyes so that they trace the shape of a figure eight lying on its side...

> Do this twenty-one times in one direction, then twenty-one times in the other. Close your eyes and say the following affirmations (three times) aloud if you can...
>
> It's ok for me to feel confused. It's ok for me to feel confused. It's ok for me to feel confused.
>
> It's ok for me to make mistakes. It's ok for me to make mistakes. It's ok for me to make mistakes.
>
> It's ok for me to feel scared. It's ok for me to feel scared. It's ok for me to feel scared.
>
> Now continue reading.

THE FABRICATION OF CONSENSUS REALITY

We are conscripted to the consensus through an innocent desire on the part of those involved in our early life and upbringing. When we arrive our carers are intent on communicating with us as new arrivals in the world. They include us in their reality, but it is very unusual for them to consider that a new arrival might inhabit a reality that could have any relevance for the carers. A condition of ignorance is assumed, and the carers' reality is forced upon the new arrival by means of the basic polarity dyad of approval and condemnation.

Only when we comply with what supports the carers' reality are our actions and expressions given any validity. As children we are conditioned in this way. As we get older we learn to call it education.

When we behave in accordance with the conditioning, the carers say we are getting along well. THEY SEE THEIR REALITY DUPLICATED IN US and make all kinds of assumptions that we see the world the same way as they do. They PROJECT their interpretation onto us simply because we behave in a way that fits their pattern, regardless of what's going on internally with us.

This can further distance us from our connection with the subtle realms. How often do children perceive something *imaginary* only to be told it is nothing when they enquire about it? A simple example would be that of a child asking its mother what the shimmering light around her head was. A response of "Oh that's nothing." tells the child that its own perception of auras is a mistake. What it thought was something is in fact nothing and therefore to be disregarded. This kind of invalidation has been identified as stifling imagination in children, but it also effectively shuts down the ability to perceive many of the phenomena of the subtle realms.

Always the internal interpretive patterns that drive the consensus projection are reinforced; anything else is consigned to insignificance – or nonsense. After a while we join the club and do exactly the same thing ourselves with our own offspring. A collective consensus reality is established that validates the existence of those who subscribe to it. It can then become very frightening – and dangerous – to deviate from this consensus or to challenge it in any way. We become part of the problem without seeing that it is a problem, and without realizing that we have any alternative.

> *The consensus reality sustains, and is sustained by,*
> *the unconscious fear of re-experiencing the trauma*
> *of separation. If we don't join [we believe] our*
> *existence is forfeit.*

What the process of projection creates for us is a situation where any convention, once adopted, is so reinforced that it becomes a dominant thought-form or mental strategy. The energy invested in this strategy then accumulates to such a degree that it marginalizes, or even obliterates, the alternatives. The origins and formulation of such strategies are then forgotten, as they become a simple matter of routine.

As long as these routines are running within me they will continue to inform my self-identity. I will continue to map my unconscious beliefs onto what I understand to be external to me, and I will continue to see the externals as the cause of my predicament.

The conclusion to be drawn from this is that we are projecting all the time. We are living in an illusion, but if we are then it is our illusion (it could even be said that we live in a delusional state). This also implies that we must be creating the reality we exist within, and this means we can change it. This is the place of personal empowerment, and it is the fundamental premise that underwrites the positive thinking self-help movement.

LIVING WITH THE ILLUSION

What we must realize with this is that the chances of moving out of illusion into a place of absolute truth through the facility of the mortal mind are zero. What we can do is move to another illusion – one that works better for us, or one we have a preference for. But we cannot really get away from the self-identity created by the mortal mind, and the dysfunctional constructs it calls reality.

This would seem to leave us stuck with the conundrum that our adopted reality cannot give us access to an object reality. We might also start to consider that true *reality* is actually a condition we have never thought of as real. We may not even be able to conceive of true reality with the mortal mind.

Another conclusion we can draw is that what we learn to call reality is a part of the separation process that disconnects us from our inherent spiritual core. Furthermore as long as we adhere to rigid concepts of objective reality we will remain in a state of disconnection. This is in no way advocating that what we experience as solid reality is disregarded; such a course of action can only lead to disaster. It is more that we be prepared to discover that nothing is as we thought it was.

This kind of thinking stretches the mortal mind to breaking point, and runs us into all of our own resistance. [You might want to revisit the eye exercise given earlier in the chapter.] However if we can live in this paradox without insisting on making anything the absolute truth, we initiate a move into self-mastery. This is a condition of being, one where we begin to understand and control our own projections and we see the projections of others coming at us. We actually begin to revert to a strange condition that existed before the mortal mind was fully activated – it is called innocence

> And [Jesus] said, Verily I say unto you, Except ye be converted, and become as little children, ye shall not enter into the kingdom of heaven. (Matthew 18:3)

Don't be put off by this quotation from the Bible. There is much written in all ancient religious texts that is relevant to the spiritual quest. Remember, it is the assumptions made in the use of language that mask the message. There is also a great deal of accumulated baggage – connotation, association and dogma – that comes with religion, none of which is relevant as it is all the product of the mortal mind. Meaning is not inscribed in the words themselves it emerges from within. Consider the difference between the above quotation and the following: *Enlightenment is achieved through a process of personal transformation that returns the mind to its original condition of innocence.* Is there any difference, and if there is what is its essence?

Whatever existed before the mortal mind was activated by

physical experience is still there. It is the consciousness that is able to observe the mortal mind in all its confusion, and is also able to watch us from inside as we act out the behavior patterns that we know hold no truth for us.

Simply knowing the existence of this observer consciousness demonstrates the *principle of separation* that the mortal mind has structured itself around. It also emphasizes any conflict between personal authenticity and the adopted self-identity.

Constant suppression of what I feel to be authentic for me is inherent in the process of creating a self-identity. It is the root of all disharmony. It engenders a deep rage inside which will sabotage me if I do not find a way to allow it to express. If I do not learn to allow this expression it will turn inwards and fester as resentment. Thereafter, it will seek to escape and will express itself in destructive forms that are contaminated with resentment and all its cohorts: fear, bitterness, control, suspicion, jealousy, hate, judgment, criticism and blame.

OTHERNESS AND ENEMY PATTERNING

Enemy patterning, or enemy programming, is the process by which we construct others as our enemies. To put it another way it's the process of identifying the antithesis of all we believe in and stand for as present in other people. We do this simply by seeing them fit into particular categories, and invoking the conventions of the reality we have adopted.

This means we project an identity onto them that has been constructed from a particular perspective that we subscribe to. This identity will have nothing to do with the other's own internal processes, and how they think about themselves. Except, if we are in a confrontational or conflict situation they will be projecting an identity on to us in a similar manner.

Everything starts from me, and my concept of who I am. Because of the way I've been conditioned I will tend to seek approval – either from myself or from some external source. Approval is the determining influence that creates the qualities of *rightness* and *wrongness, goodness* and *badness.*

My concept of who I am is essentially a view of myself – and how I fit into the world I perceive around me. It's who I think I am. Anything I detect that conflicts with this self-identity my mind has created will be seen as a threat to my existence. This includes any thoughts I have and observations I make about myself that bring my assumed self-identity into question. I internalize these as what I am not. They can never be accepted as relating to me in any way, so I will place these offending qualities outside and separate from me. I determine that they can only exist external to me. I will attempt to attribute them to someone or something else. The projection process then works something like this:

- I construct my identity as someone who is good, and justify myself through approval.
- If I am good, what is bad cannot be me; what is bad cannot exist where I exist.
- Therefore what is bad can only exist where I "am not".
- If I discover something within me that I don't like – and this includes anything that doesn't fit in with the reality I've created for myself – I will want to pretend it isn't there. It is not who I have decided I am, therefore I cannot possibly admit to its existence in me. I deny it.
- What cannot exist within me can only exist outside me – where I "am not".
- Where I "am not" is the realm of the other – everyone else (and everything else) who is not me.
- The mental process of association, one of the fundamental operations of the mind, then easily subsumes equivalences between what is "not me", what is wrong and what is bad. All of this is part of one enormous subset of the entirety of creation – THE REST OF IT.
- From everyone else's perspective you are a part of that subset – a part of the rest of creattion.
- This means that everyone else is potentially a representative of what is bad, and by implication bad in themselves. They are all

then available for me to project any of my unacceptable qualities – my badness – onto. They are all potential enemies!

This was well demonstrated in a group seminar I facilitated in Cork (Republic of Ireland). At one point one participant, Nigel, was complaining about another participant, Rosemary. Nigel was saying how he always felt judged and inadequate around Rosemary, and whatever it was she was doing he wanted her to stop it. He was in fact desperately trying to get her attention, and approval, but pretending otherwise. Without any intervention from me, Rosemary looked Nigel straight in the eye and said: "What's happening here, Nigel, is that you've got several problems and you want to call them all Rosemary."

Identification Exercise
1. List all the qualities you believe are good about yourself.
2. List all the qualities you believe are bad about yourself.
3. List all the positive human qualities that you believe you lack.
4. List all the negative human qualities you believe you could never have, or express.

At the end of the chapter you will find a commentary on these beliefs. The indication it gives about how you identify yourself in the world may surprise you.

RESPONSIBILITY

Whatever my background circumstances, because of the existential paradigm of approval that permeates the culture I live in I will endeavor to conceptualize myself as *good* and *right*. Consequently I will seek to justify myself and rationalize any faults I perceive in the way I present myself to the world.

Therefore, any time I catch myself defending or justifying myself I can be sure that I've found some anomaly in my world context, and my position in it, that threatens to destabilize the identity I've constructed for myself. This means my reality is under threat. When this happens watch out for major emotional eruptions.

The real gift in this is that suddenly my projection becomes a tool for my growth, rather than a vice that I must seek to avoid – or at least avoid being caught out in. Projection may not be a virtue, but it is only a vice if I see it that way and fail to understand it as a basic characteristic of my humanness that I can embrace and take advantage of.

Once I know that I project, and come to a place of acceptance with this idea, I am at a point of power. I am in a position to revise my entire concept of myself and how I express in life. I can choose to continue as before, or to change. The *principle of responsibility* comes into effect here, because in the moment I choose consciously whether to change or continue as I have been it is no longer possible for me to blame my condition on anyone else.

I have become responsible for myself, because I know that if I continue as before I have chosen to deny myself the opportunity of a fuller expression of my being. If, knowing this, I am content I am still in a place of consciousness. If, however, I find myself in conflict with myself then I know that my energy is being misdirected. I can then choose again how to continue. Either way I am exercising conscious responsibility, and I am empowered.

REFLECTION – AS WITHIN SO WITHOUT

If I regard my external world as a reflection of my internal process, I can learn a lot about myself. At a basic level there are clear correlations: if my home is untidy it's likely that my thinking is untidy; if my home is super-tidy it's likely that my thinking is over-controlled; if my home is crowded with objects then it's likely that I have accumulated emotional baggage. But be very clear the examples given here are only potentials – they are interpretations not absolute truth.

The reflection process is just that, a process; it is not static. What means one thing today can mean another tomorrow. I have to learn to interrogate my situation and read the messages. This is a matter of understanding what I create with my unconscious thought patterns through the *principle of creation and manifestation.*

The major precept of the *principle of creation and manifestation* is that I create what I focus my energy and my thought on. So I know I must focus on what I want rather than on what I don't want. If what is manifesting in my life is what I don't want then the inference is that somewhere inside I am focused on what I don't want. This is where the concept of reflection, as discussed here, can be of immense value.

When something that I don't want appears in my life my first response is to acknowledge it and accept it. Whatever it is it has the potential to show me something I was unaware of up until the point when it appeared. The next step is to deal with any practical necessities. Then it's time to move out of the victimhood of *Why has this happened to me?* into the more constructive *What is there for me to learn from this situation?*

Whenever we ask a question of this kind we always receive an answer. Sometimes the answer comes through the external world and sometimes from the internal. However as the external is a reflection of the internal the source is really the same; it is from the *Universe* operating through the *principles of universal wisdom, and information and in-tuition.* The key is to develop an alertness to listen for the answers.

Some time ago I returned home from a trip abroad to find my flat had been burgled in my absence. This was an immense shock. I couldn't understand how I had attracted this experience into my life, but because of the principles I live by I knew such a traumatic event held an important message for me. So once the practical side of things was dealt with, I meditated deeply on what I was being shown. What I came up with was as follows:

> I live modestly by western standards, in an ordinary area of London with my wife. Neither of us engages with materialistic icons of success. We are both creative and we enjoy the audio and visual arts. I believed we had little of value to steal. Yet what was taken was exactly what we valued: CD collection, musical instruments and a collection of classic movies accumulated over years.

We went away without securing our home. The back door was left unlocked – as it had been habitually for a long time – and this would have invalidated any insurance had we had any in place. The clear message to me was that I did not value myself, had never valued myself, and it was time to change this pattern in myself. The message for my wife was similar, and we saw it as an area where we both supported each other's dysfunction.

When I reflected deeper on this I saw that in some ways I had never held myself in very high esteem. I reckoned that if I could do something anyone could do it. I still believe this to a degree, but I had a mind-set that said there was value only in rarity and scarcity. What this meant was that I had been living my life without ever giving myself credit for anything I'd achieved. I'd seen myself as having no value. This insight was stunning, and it held a lot of answers to the questions of why certain things in my life were as they were. It showed me where to focus my intent in order to create a major shift in my personal circumstances.

This particular story is of a significant personal incident, but the same principles can be applied to the smallest discomfort. Sometimes the little things help us to learn sufficiently so that we can avoid more destructive events. This is particularly true of personal relationships. Whenever someone produces a reaction in you remember that it is you who is reacting, so you are responsible. Ask yourself what you are reacting to deep down. Ask yourself how this person is showing you something you don't like about yourself, or something that you've changed in yourself because you didn't like it. Ask yourself what the judgment is that you hold around the person, the attitude or the action. And remember that all interpretations must ultimately come from you, even though you may seek assistance in making that interpretation. There are no maybes and possibles to this; it must feel as if it fits.

TAKING THINGS PERSONALLY

Now it's time to look at what happens when we notice issues in others and when others tell us about our own issues; bear in mind that to everyone else you are the other. A good general rule would be to stop looking at the faults in other people; you give them energy and reinforce them by doing this. You especially aggravate the situation if you give expression to what you see as a fault.

In my seeking to evolve consciously I sometimes invite input from other people in the form of feedback. What I have to remember is that when I ask for this I provide them with an opportunity to project their issues, their judgments and their expectations onto me. No matter how hard they try, they will never be able to completely exclude these items from their feedback. But this does not make the feedback redundant; it just means I have to be conscious of my reaction to it.

Sometimes I can be locked into a blind spot where I feel stuck and unable to feel where my focus is needed. This happens to everybody. It is then that having something pointed out to me can be of assistance as long as I remember that it is not personal and I do not take it personally. This is difficult for us all because we are such very sensitive beings – far more sensitive than is realized – and we have a habit of taking things personally.

> *Criticism is the mask of self-justification.*
> *All criticism is about the critic, and relevant to the*
> *critic alone.*

If I take something personally there is no way forward for me until I acknowledge that my internalization is simply a function of the beliefs and values I have incorporated into the self-identity I've adopted. This is true whether I feel insulted or exulted. My reaction is the surest signal of my misinterpretation of myself, and that my mortal mind is well and truly in control. My ego is either trampled or fed, neither is healthy.

If the person pointing out an issue loads their expression with their own personal judgment – and this is what usually happens, albeit unconsciously – then it is contaminated with their pain. When this happens it is very difficult for me to acknowledge my own denial even if it is present. I feel the emotional charge of the other person and the tendency is for me to identify this in some way as mine, and because I do not want to feel this, my tendency will be to close down, withdraw and become defensive.

However it's not impossible to disengage from my personal reactions when I am given feedback, it just takes practice. What I must remember is that anything delivered to me in a judgmental form telling me what I need to correct in myself is about the other person, particularly if it comes without my invitation. Without invitation whatever I'm told about my own shortcomings is totally irrelevant in the moment of telling, although it may be something I need to take account of at another time. If I get into defending myself I give energy to the other person's projection.

In fact whenever our issues are pointed out to us – as they often are when other people begin to feel insecure – it is nearly always a matter of projection. But because there is something in the projection that matches our own inner criticism of ourselves we feel exposed, vulnerable and attacked. This is never healing, but it is the way people generally operate in the world.

The dynamics and the effects of projection (and introjection) are rooted in the unconscious manipulation of energies. It is actually a violation of sovereignty – the right to individual self-determination – to offer criticism without invitation. And because this violence goes unrecognized it is suppressed in the most complacent unconscious way. The collective effect of such suppression in global terms is monumental, and it is played out on the killing fields of the various trouble spots in the world. The consequences of projection without awareness cannot be underestimated.

It seems to me to be vital that anyone in a position of leadership (politicians, negotiators, facilitators, therapists, teachers etc.) is conscious of the projection phenomenon. However a very brief consideration of the general situation shows us that there is some way to go before we see this as part of our everyday culture.

PRACTICAL

If you want to begin using your projection mechanism as a tool for your personal growth and evolution the following list summarizes the central tenets to be observed:

- It's pretty safe to assume that I project all the time, and so does everybody else.
- All personal criticism is a function of projection. Criticism is always about the critic. It is therefore irrelevant to me.
- If I find any criticism relevant it means that I carry an unconscious wound or belief that has been triggered. Criticism that comes from someone else is about them. Criticism from myself (self-criticism) indicates that I have failed to match up to some internal standard. It may serve me to investigate where or who that standard originates from, and how I have absorbed it into my reality.
- Whenever I feel an emotional charge in relation to another's actions or comments I know that I've found a key to a deeper level of understanding of myself.
- If I feel anything other than a compassionate internal response to any comment directed at me, or if I get into a defensive form of expression, then I have an issue somewhere that may need attention.
- If I find myself judging or criticizing someone else I know that I am projecting, and there is something for me to look at in myself.
- Whenever I recoil from something in my external world I know it somehow reflects something within me that I need to understand and accept, and possibly address with transformational intent.
- Whatever I reject in my world is a reflection of what I judge and reject in myself.
- Whenever I feel pained, disappointed, aggrieved, resentful, saddened (or satisfied, elated, reassured) by the remarks or behavior of another I have invested my energy in them – given my power away – which means I have been projecting.
- Whenever I take something personally I have switched unconsciously into defense mode. Somewhere in this process there will be a denial although it may not be directly related to the

incident that produced the defensiveness. But it means that I have taken on a projection somewhere – maybe in the past – which is producing a sense of insecurity.

- Whenever I take something personally it is really only a reminder of somewhere that I refuse to love myself. It is a signal that is all; and I have the opportunity to choose to do something about it or not.
- Whenever I express myself in terms of what *I am not* I am in denial. This is inherent in the linguistic structure of negation and was identified very clearly by Freud[f] in his seminal works on psychoanalysis. If I am not projecting in the statement of my denial, the chances are that I will move into projection with the very next utterance.
- Whenever I come across an incidence of projection I have been presented with an opportunity to heal a wound that has been buried under layers of coping strategies and programming.
- Projection is ok; it is my interpretation of it and the significance I attach to this that is the problem – my problem.

Some experimentation may be needed with where and what you feel in situations where projection is flying around. My experience of being projected onto produces a feeling of tension in my solar plexus in particular, but also in my chest and shoulders – areas that protect my heart center.

When I project something from my own shadow – that well of darkness where I hide what I don't want to believe about myself – I feel a tightening in my heart. This comes with a sense of not liking myself very much which tells me I've acted in a way that is not congruent with who I am. This contrasts with the feeling of strength and compassion that accompanies staying in integrity with my own center.

In personal exchanges when someone is projecting onto me there will be all kinds of shifting and positioning trying to blame me for their feelings and draw me into a discussion in defense of my actions and comments. Conversely when I feel an impulse to get into guilt and shame, yet stay connected with myself there is an inner recognition that I have made progress; and I feel strong.

The more you practice, the more you will find that you are continually learning to stay centered in all kinds of situations. This is an ongoing educational process that I once thought I would come to the end of. I now realize there is always more of my authentic self to be drawn out and the entire field and dynamic of projection serve this purpose. I trust you will come to realize the same for yourself.

Disengaging from Personal Criticism

When I feel under attack from the personal criticism and judgment of other people the first thing I have to do is recognize what I am feeling, identify it in some way. I am then able to say to myself *this is an attack*. I make a point of accepting that regardless of what is happening nobody really wants to be attacking me, and if they are it's because they're in pain.

Once I have made this identification I know that it has nothing to do with me. The attack is all about the fear present in the attacker. One of the most powerful ways to counter this is to open my heart and send love to the attacker. Let's be clear here; this is not accepting the violation and supporting the attack. It's recognizing that under the attack is pain and fear, and underneath that is a soul like me doing its absolute best to cope with something it finds extremely difficult. Even if I cannot feel compassion in the situation I can at least understand, and intend to be compassionate. My intent in this will do the work.

This practice of sending love and compassion to an adversary can produce miraculous changes. Try it, you've got nothing to loose. If it doesn't work, it doesn't matter. But if it works you've engaged with your *Spiritual Intelligence* in a remarkably practical way.

Identification Exercise Commentary

1. The qualities you believe are good about yourself represent what you think you are.
2. The qualities you believe are bad about yourself also represent what you think you are, and what you wish you were not.
3. All the positive human qualities you believe you lack are an

indication of how you reject and criticize yourself.
4. All the negative human qualities you believe you could never have represent how you reject others. These qualities are also what you fear to discover in yourself, and so fuel your denial and projection process.

All of these beliefs are what you are up against in your day-to-day existence. They limit your expression as a vehicle of universal consciousness.

Letting Go Of Criticism

Judgment and criticism is a violation. I know this from my own experience of being criticized, and although I may want to pre-empt and prevent any criticism from being directed at me the real issue is for me to stop the judgmental process in myself. I will never be able to prevent other people interpreting my thoughts, words and actions as criticism; but I can change my judgmental habits.

If I want to let go of these behavior patterns and avoid inflicting my pain on anyone else, I need to see where I engage in it. I need to see where I support the critical process in myself. Whenever I accept judgment or criticism I unconsciously and inherently support the violation – but defending myself is NOT the way to return the energy to its source. The energy returns naturally to its source when there is nothing in me for it to stick to – i.e. when I have no reaction.

However it is not sufficient to program myself to be non-reactive, that does nothing except lock me in tighter to the control strategies of my mortal mind. Furthermore it numbs out my feeling ability and disconnects me from my essence. If I want to free myself from the tyranny of my emotional reactions and critical responses it is imperative that I search out the primary causes. Then I must accept what I find and be present with it.

The *Emotional Tie-Cutting* procedures given in chapter nine are excellent for releasing projections taken on from others in relationships, families, school, peer groups and social interactions of every kind. But there is a foundation process that is more appropriate to begin with. This is more a reclamation of our own energy, than a rejection of the energy of another. To use this, take yourself into a centered space as indicated in the earlier chapters. Then speak the following aloud:

> ⮑ Spirit, please work with me at every level Physical, Mental, Emotional and Spiritual, ... Work holographically throughout all lifetimes, all realities, all dimensions and forms of existence ... and work with my Cellular Memory ... my Ancestral Memory ... my Soul Memory (Akashic Record) ...
>
> [Work also with my mind and mental body, and my emotional body]
>
> I <insert full name> recall to me all the critical energy that I have ever projected into the world ... all the resentment ... all the blame ... all the disappointment ... all the expectation ... all the shame ... all the fear ... all the malice ... and any other malignant or life-degrading force I have ever originated ...
>
> I reclaim this energy now ... It is mine ... and I direct that it is revealed to me in the most appropriate form and timing to be embraced, re-absorbed and transmuted into Divine Love, Divine Light, Divine Truth and Divine Wisdom ...
>
> Work with anyone else involved ... to remove these energies from every aspect of their being ... and bring them to a place of balance in the optimum way for them.
>
> Melt away all the tension, trauma, fear, pain, shame and despair ... any of this has ever created in me ... and transmute all of these energies into Divine Love, Divine Light, Divine Truth and Divine Wisdom also ... [... other qualities like compassion, expression, passion, freedom etc. can be included here...]

Have no expectation with this exercise, but be prepared for anything. Thoughts and emotions can arise from incidents you thought you'd dealt with, but had really just pushed away. With anything that comes up stay present and allow it to come out. Keep your body as open as possible and breathe as deeply as you can. What you feel in these instances is what is leaving. If you stop it you simply trap the old pain in your body once more.

7.
Being Embodied

Now it's time to talk about what it means to *be* in your body. This is a strange concept for most people when they first encounter it. Isn't the fact that you're alive here and now proof that you are in your body? Well maybe, but I want to approach this from the standpoint of considering where your energy is centered in your body, and whether you are actually in your body at all. The fact that you are walking around and functioning physically is no evidence of this

What does it mean to be aware of where your energy is centered in your body? What is your energy anyway?

Your energy is the dynamic essence of your spirit in action. It is the essence of your presence, the substance that animates you and gives you life. The place where your energy is centered in your body is the place you act from. This may not be where you think it is, and if you're not used to feeling where your energy is it may take a little perseverance to get a sense of it.

The written or printed word is not the best medium for achieving this sense, as the reading process tends to center the energy in the mortal mind – which corresponds physically to the head. However most people can relate to experiences they would have called heart-warming, on the one hand, and panic on the other. These are extremes that illustrate the movement of personal energy within the body. A heart-warming sense is only possible when your energy is centered in your body. Panic and its associate terror are symptoms that your energy is moving out of your body. These are interesting indicators that reflect the level of integration of body and spirit.

There is a tension that arises out of a lack of centeredness. This comes from the consciousness of the body itself, which feels the reluctance of the spiritual essence within to fully inhabit the physical vehicle. The underlying fear of the body is that the essence will depart completely, the body will be abandoned and die.

When your energy is fully centered in your body you are naturally relaxed, when your energy is only partially present in your center you are tense. This is true whether you are aware of it or not.

When your energy is absent from your center – that is to say when it is operating through another area of your physicality – you will be imbalanced, even to the point of serious dysfunction. Of course, this is likely to seem perfectly normal to you as this is the background condition that informs your concept of reality and your self-identity. It will only become a conscious aspect of your existence if and when you begin to consider how satisfied you are with the way things are in your life.

UNCONSCIOUSNESS

There are many levels of unconsciousness, all created by the mortal mind. This is an effect that will be obscured by false beliefs and mental constructs masquerading as rationalization and clear logic. However it is to be remembered that one of the characteristics of the mortal mind is that it constructs its own logic based on hidden assumptions which are derived from its own explanations to itself of the sensory and feeling input generated by the experience of physical existence. The mind may think that *it* is the seat of consciousness; however that is a very good reason in itself to doubt the reliability of any such belief.

Most of the time your attention will be focused in the past, or the future; engaged in moving toward, or away from, some situation or other that diverts your attention from where you are in the moment. When this is the case your energy is not in your center.

When you are focused in the future you are mentally driven. It feels like you don't have time for yourself, as if you have to put your needs aside and get on with things. This can become so habitual that you don't even notice that you're living in this way. And if you do notice, maybe you promise yourself that you'll take time out and relax, when everything is done. In this state you are not really living, but existing.

When you are focused in the past you are emotionally driven. The future disappears along with the present. It feels as if there isn't much point in doing anything. This leads very quickly to depression, which again can go unnoticed and accepted as a habitual way of being. If you find yourself going through the motions of day-to-day survival serving out a life sentence of drudgery it's highly likely that you are operating in a depressed condition, even though you may hide this from yourself. Again this is existence rather than living.

If your energy is not in your center, the obvious question to ask is where is it? Well, your energy tends to rise up in your body according to your level of disconnection from the moment. You can do a very easy check on this by speaking aloud; note where the power of your voice seems to come from in your body. Where does it resonate?

This test has nothing to do with the pitch of your voice, or the physical location of your vocal chords. It concerns where you *feel* the power of your voice to be coming from in your body. This is a guide to where your energy is sitting. If your voice seems to come from your throat (or above) your energy is not in your body.

In reality our energy tends to be dynamically distributed, depending on the level of unconscious fear we are carrying. We are not dealing with a black and white phenomenon, so the voice test is not an absolute measurement, but it is a good way to begin monitoring where our energy sits within ourselves.

The commonest place for your energy to withdraw to is your head. This is what is meant by the phrase *being in your head*. It is the condition where your energy is centered in your brain, and your mortal mind is actively in control of you. In this state your breathing is shallow, your body is tense and your feelings closed down. This condition prevails throughout most of modern society and is sustained by the privileging of intellectual thought and mental agility.

In some social circles the term *being in your head* is used disparagingly. We hear it as a criticism applied to anyone whose ideas seem to be strung together in a complexity that only they understand. It is also an indication that thinking and talking are being used to avoid feeling. It is worth noting here that all criticism comes from being in the head and is rooted in the *principle of projection*. The fact that the expression *being in your head* is in use pejoratively in this way is also an indication that somewhere within, in the generally un-accessed regions of the mind, resides the knowing that being in your center (*Tan Tien*) is more supportive of life.

When you are in your head, you are actually in a state of *un*consciousness even though your mind may be very active – a notion that might be difficult to understand initially. The unconsciousness comes from the fact that you are constantly engaged in thinking. Your awareness is focused on results – either those you have produced, or those you want to produce. The consequence of this is that your life runs to a preconceived agenda, a program – what your mind has determined your reaction to your circumstances *should* be.

This is never a measured response to the experience of the moment. It's about what will appear to be right, what will gain you approval, what you already know, what you think will get you what you want, what you think will keep you safe. And wherever the agenda is not met there is stress, regret, mental anguish, and suffering.

Consider the following everyday situations: walking to the shops; driving; your journey to work; eating; drinking; taking part in some physical activity; making love; ironing; cooking; cleaning the house. What is your mind doing while your body is engaged in these things? What is it planning? What is it worrying about? Where is it trying to get to? What is it fantasizing about? What is it telling you that you are doing wrong? If your mind is doing anything other than focusing on where you are in the moment, and what you are feeling, your energy is in your head. The everyday term for this kind of behavior is distraction; you are elsewhere.

> *Whenever you are not present to yourself you are*
> *unconscious.*

MAKING IT SAFE

The main reason for your energy to be in your head is that it's where everyone else here operates from. So your place in the scheme of things could be under serious threat, if you fail to match them. This is a reason, and not the cause. Sooner or later this situation unconsciously maps onto your core separation trauma and reinforces some aspect of abandonment, worthlessness or rejection – which doesn't mean that you have to be feeling abandoned or rejected or feel worthless. It could be you doing the abandoning and rejecting, which always implies a projected lack of worth. It's the core separation trauma that is the ultimate difficulty.

As we've already seen, this trauma is largely created out of an illusion of misinterpretation. It is then compounded by any difficulty in material circumstances – and in cases where people are born into extreme situations the misinterpretation is easily justified.

It is not a crime to be in your head. It's simply a mode of existence adopted because it appears to be the only option. The main conclusion the mind draws, from its interpretation of the co-incidence of birth and everything else that was perceived at the time, is that it's not safe to be here in the world. That means it's not safe to be in our bodies. The curious thing about this is that we actually gather the information that guides us in establishing our relationships through feeling. Just consider this for a while.

When you interact with another person...

- Do you assess the level of openness or vulnerability that is safe for you to maintain?
- Do you assess the level of openness or vulnerability in the other person?
- Do feel relieved if you find the other person expresses similarly to you?
- Do you feel anxious if you find the other person seems to be more physical, or more mental than you?

These are all ways in which you use your feeling (and intuition) to guide you, and keep you safe. You might also like to consider exactly what your process is in these situations, especially if you often have the experience of going against your intuition to your cost. Try an experiment of acting on your feeling more and see what happens. At first do this only in situations where the outcome is not critical so there is no charge of anxiety attached to the process. Then if you find that the results are favorable try it out in riskier ways.

When we incarnate we are a mass of feeling, yet somehow we can feel that all around us is a fear of feeling. This is determined through the *principle of interconnection* and the *principle of in-formation and intuition*. As those around us are already experienced in the physical world the assumption is that they know something we don't.

The body is the part of us that feels. If it's not safe to feel neither can it be safe to be in the body. So the conclusion of the mortal mind is that it's not safe here. The mind is determined to keep us safe. It has also determined that the body is the place of feeling and feeling is dangerous. This gives us a self-sustaining closed loop that disconnects us from our bodies. The body is objectified and alienated.

If we are feeling we must be in our bodies, but through convention we have learned to reject many of our feelings simply because they are uncomfortable and we don't like them. They remind us of the experience of incarnation and all the pain and confusion associated with that. So we refuse to feel certain aspects of our existence – or refuse to acknowledge what we feel.

However if we revert to our feelings a curious anomaly arises.

We have determined that the people forming our social order are not in their bodies through the *principle of interconnection*. We can feel when there's no-one there, so we know there's no point in going there ourselves. We will simply feel the isolation more intensely if we do, and this will reinforce our core separation trauma. This means that OUR FEELING IS KEEPING US SAFE. But the mortal-mind overlooks this as it undermines the belief that feelings have little value. The truth is that our feeling will always keep us safe, but the mind will override our feeling with logic, often disastrously.

The mind uses mental strategies designed to numb us out and give us a sense of being safe. The mortal mind actually believes it's looking after us in adopting this process, and in some ways it is because if we don't fit in we are likely to suffer rejection from our peers. However, each apparently successful strategy reinforces the mind's belief in itself and its ability to control its existence. This is the manner whereby our energy leaves the body and comes under the control of the mortal mind.

When you are in your head you are thinking all the time. In this condition your attention is elsewhere, no matter what you are doing. This means your energy is focused elsewhere. You cannot therefore be fully present to your experience.

We actually disconnect from our inner selves whenever we remain in a situation that stresses us out knowing, or believing, that we should leave. We retreat into our intellect, into our imaginings, into the head. This is a self-preservation pattern we adopt to disconnect from our feelings in situations where we seem to be trapped. Recognizing that we cannot leave physically we withdraw mentally. This is the only way we can hang-out in an environment we find toxic; we pretend to ourselves that we are not there. When we do this for long enough it becomes a life-strategy. We learn to live outside ourselves all the time. In this state we are seldom present with ourselves or anybody else; there's nobody home. This is endemic in the consensus reality of western society.

Whenever you operate from your mortal mind alone you are disconnected from the moment, and you cannot respond effectively to any situation you find yourself in. There are several factors that contribute to this situation. The first has already been mentioned – the preference given to all forms of rationalization and intellectualism. However this masks the deeper truth that the mortal mind is a *virtual entity* that has taken control of you. Moreover the moment you start to really feel what's going on in and around you the mind immediately gives you a rush of fear.

Alarming though this might sound, it is not so terrible. The mortal mind is a powerful instrument that few have learned to use. It is not dysfunctional, nor is it your enemy. It is simply out of control. The trouble with the mortal mind is it thinks it is you, so it thinks by keeping itself safe it keeps you safe. Also it thinks it understands itself, but it is completely self-identified, which means its identity is sustained only within its own thought process. This identity is artificial in every respect, but it is nevertheless determined survive.

The strategy for this is simple. The mortal mind hijacks your feelings. Your body's basic survival responses are used as blueprints for emotional programming, which your mind creates to divert your attention from what it fears – annihilation.

Any time the self-identified existence of the mortal mind comes under threat the impending danger is translated into a physical response; up pops the fear of annihilation hiding behind the body's imperative to survive. This can be very uncomfortable as the mortal mind is capable of triggering extreme terror by giving the body the message that it's about to die. With practice you can watch this happening. Wherever you feel this sudden terror in your body – the surges, the impulses, the tingling or the numbness is an indication of how your mortal mind has appropriated the responses of your body's energy system.

THE NATURAL CENTER AND THE ENERGY SYSTEM

Traditional eastern philosophies and martial arts offer several models for the energy system of the body. Few aspects of these find favor with western scientific materialism; however they do have a certain relevance when considering energy as a spiritual phenomenon.

Because of the lack of a consensus acceptance in western cultures of the concept of the human body (or anything else) as an energy system, there is no linguistic convention to describe it. There are very strong eastern traditions, however, that do have the linguistic facility to accommodate these concepts. Consequently the most usual way to describe the human energy system is in terms of chakras.

Chakra is the Sanskrit word for wheel. It is used to refer to energy centers in the body because when seen psychically that is how they appear. For simplicity I like to adopt a basic model that sees seven main chakras located along the line of the spine. The chakras have the job of drawing energy into the body from the *Universal Field of Consciousness* acting as a connection between physical and subtle aspects. With a certain amount of overlap, they can be related to specific functions at physical, emotional, mental and spiritual levels.

The first, or root, chakra lies at the base of the body, at the perineum – between the anus and the scrotum in men, and the anus and the vagina in women. This chakra relates to the most basic survival instincts and needs of the body, staying alive (at the expense of others if necessary): physical vitality, food, safety, shelter and the family, grounding and connection with the earth.

The second, or sacral, chakra is a short distance up the body from the root chakra in the region between the navel and the perineum. This chakra relates to issues of personal expression: creativity, sexuality, purpose, personal identity and group membership, which frequently evolve into ideas of elitism and superiority. It resonates strongly with the emotional body, the repository of the pain of the past.

The third, or solar plexus, chakra is located at the base of the sternum – the breastbone. This chakra is the seat of the ego, it relates to issues of personal power: status, control, ownership, intellect and individuality, these often manifest as the desire to own or possess, and the desire to be seen as significant in the world. It resonates strongly with the mental body, the mind's intermediary for controlling the emotional body through worry (fear of the future).

The fourth, or heart, chakra is located in the region of the physical

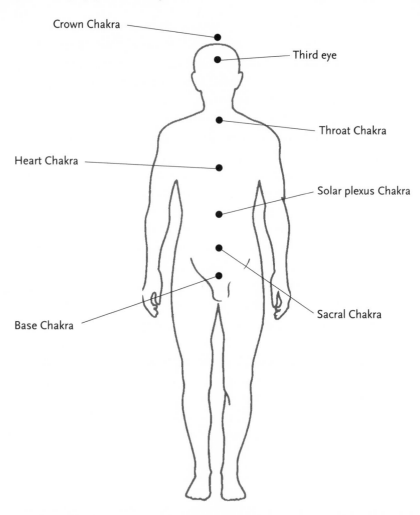

heart, but is actually in the center of the chest. This chakra relates to issues of being, authenticity, integrity and truth. It is the center of *Spiritual Intelligence* in the body, and the source of manifestation.

The fifth, or throat chakra, is located in the area of the voice box. This chakra relates to communication and self-expression. It reflects the conditions prevailing in the lower three chakras, particularly the solar plexus. Whatever you consider to be your truth finds expression through this chakra; this truth is totally conditioned by your beliefs about yourself and the unresolved issues of your lower chakras.

The sixth chakra, or third eye, is located inside the brain at a level that corresponds to the middle of the forehead. This chakra relates to vision, essentially creative vision, the process of translating that vision into physical reality and the perception of truth. This chakra also reflects the conditions prevalent in the lower three chakras particularly the sacral. Your perception of truth is clouded by any fears and false beliefs held in the lower three chakras.

The seventh, or crown chakra, is located at the top of the head vertically above the spinal column. This chakra relates to spiritual connection and universal wisdom. It is the transpersonal doorway that opens onto oneness with all.

According to eastern traditions the natural center for your energy is the *Tan Tien*. This is an area in the lower abdomen just below the navel. It is somewhere between the solar plexus and the pubic bone, in some Chinese systems it's known as the *triple-warmer* as it draws on the energy of the lower three chakras – solar plexus, sacral and root.

When your energy is centered here it feels natural, and you feel connected to your body and the world around you. Your body is strong in this condition and your mind alert, yet relaxed. You are grounded and present. You are in the moment – the Now. One way to describe this condition is that you feel calm and alert, in control; you are ready to respond instantly to any situation or event. Most people have some sense of being in this condition at various times in their lives, but it is not generally an everyday experience. The simplest procedure to begin bringing your energy into your center is the process given in the practical section at the end of chapter one.

MOVING FROM HEAD TO HEART

What actually happens with your energy is that the location of its focus within you is constantly readjusting itself. Where it is settled in any one moment is dependent how safe you feel in your body at the time, and this is dependent upon the programs your mind is running and your level of engagement with them.

All effective personal development work functions to engage with the *principle of alignment*, and to shift your energy within you so that you can live in a more balanced way. It helps you to disengage from the mental and emotional programs run by the mortal mind. In general what tends to happen is that your awareness is coaxed out of your head towards your heart, the aim being to bring your energy into your heart center and encourage you to operate from there.

There is a lot of value in this. As you begin to feel what it's like to be centered in your heart there is an expansion of consciousness within you, but it is still only half of the equation. What really needs to happen is that you must learn to hold your energy in your center (*Tan Tien*) in all conditions; this is where the feelings are buried. As the issues that relate to your buried feelings are cleared your energy will naturally begin to expand and express through your heart center – more about this in the next chapter.

None of this can be done by will-power alone; the mortal mind is very good at convincing you that you are centered in your heart. Moving into your heart centre can only be achieved through giving intent and committing to be present with whatever surfaces in the process, surrendering any agenda you might have thought up about how things are supposed to be. But it is a two-way street. The more you live in integrity with yourself, with your true feelings and face up to your challenges, the more your energy will gravitate to your center and the more you will operate through your heart naturally. It will greatly assist your progress in this regard to learn to observe yourself in a detached manner.

THE WITNESS STATE

If you can begin to observe yourself reacting you invoke the *principle of self-awareness*, and you will enter the *witness* state. This is very in-teresting, because another level of consciousness becomes apparent here. It is one of the places your mortal mind will not want you to go, so it will not co-operate easily. You will find yourself suddenly think-ing about your sanity and various potential personality disorders.

The witness state starts to appear as you question yourself – question your thoughts, and your mind. It is more apparent in times of severe stress and conflict. If you can hear, or see, yourself arguing with yourself inside you're onto it, because there will be at least two voices inside your head. The interesting question is: *who do these voices belong to?* And even more interesting is *who is listening to these voices? Who is watching what's going on?* If the observer (listener and watcher) is you who or what are the others?

The observer is who you really are – the essence that resides in your body. Everything else is a false you, a substitute created by your mortal mind to represent you to yourself. In your mind you are identified with the mental construct of this representation. Because there is so little understanding of this, and whatever there was is long forgotten, the mortal mind can be quite de-stabilized by the appearance of the watcher within.

> *The existence and experience of the witness state*
> *haunts the mortal mind*

The acquisition of language, and the pronoun we use to refer to ourselves – namely "I" – compound this process. Prior to this, children tend to communicate telepathically via feeling and empathy – the *principle of interconnection* – and this is superseded by language, which from the point of its acquisition on is privileged as the only legitimate way to communicate.

Language is the primary medium we use to express our thoughts. The mind hears itself called "I", and the watcher understands that "I" refers to itself (yourself). The overall effect is that you assume an equivalence, and thence identify, with your mind.

Every "I" statement you make reinforces this identification, especially if it is an "I am" statement, as when you say, "I am" you acknowledge yourself as being. Any time you say, "I am..." and predicate this with something else you are identifying yourself to yourself as that predicate. What's more you are affirming this to yourself. This is particularly disempowering in the case of emotions. When you say *I'm angry, I'm upset,* etc. you identify yourself in that moment as the emotion. The emotion is actually your mind's reaction to something you feel.

You are neither your thoughts nor your emotions. Once you enter the witness state this becomes clearer. In the witness state you are in a position to choose whether to hold on to the false identity of the mind – live a lie, or surrender this and explore the true nature of your being. You are in a position to exercise the *principle of responsibility*.

In the witness state you have dis-identified with your mind. Your breathing relaxes, and your energy begins to settle lower in your body. Because of this, the witness state also allows your feelings to be present. Your mind will still produce its reactions, but if you can practice being the witness these will have less power over you. The more you allow your feelings to be there, especially when they are intense, the clearer your emotional body will become. However, even though the mortal mind knows any self-representation is its own creation (this is inherent in the *principle of self-identity*), so much of your existence is invested in the idea of the reality of your self-identity that letting go of your belief in it can be a shattering experience.

CLEARING YOUR EMOTIONS

You will find that, as well as giving respite from emotional reactions, going into the witness state is a good way to engage consciously with your emotional clearing. Clearing your emotions cannot be avoided, if you are on a path of conscious evolution and aspiring to embody as much of your *Spiritual Intelligence* as you can. It will actually proceed in an unconscious manner if you work on opening your upper chakras without paying any attention to the issues of the chakras below your heart.

Clearing is facilitated by your breath. When you are in the witness state, you are in your body (your energy is more centered) and your feelings will surface automatically. All you have to do is remain present with them, and the best way to do this is through your breath. When you focus on your breath you cannot help but be present.

To engage with your emotional clearing, first center yourself, as described earlier in chapter four. Next create a sacred space for yourself using the following form.

> ➤ I {insert name in current use}, incarnated as {insert full birth name}, call to me the infinite resource of all that I am under **Universal Law**; and I now give intent that I remember and reclaim the sovereignty and integrity of my being and bodies as a Divine expression of **Universal Consciousness**. I call upon the **Essence of my Presence, my Guides** and **the Intelligence of Spirit** at the **Highest Level of the Light** to support and facilitate this process in me ... and I give thanks that this is so.
>
> I invite any being or consciousness of the Light, who has experience and expertise in the areas relevant to me in this moment, to be with me working through me bringing guidance, direction and support. And I particularly ask the Consciousness of ... [insert the name of any guide(s) who you relate to strongly] for assistance with this.
>
> And throughout this process I ask that the space I occupy, this room, be completely filled and surrounded with Divine Love, Divine Light, Divine Truth and Divine Wisdom.

Next say...

> Spirit, please work with me at every level: physical, emotional, mental and spiritual. Assist me now to transform and release the most appropriate layers of EMOTIONAL PROGRAMMING that I carry, which cause me to identify with my mind, and which prevent me from embodying and expressing the truth of my being. Work especially with my mind, my mental body and my emotional body, and transmute any energies released into Divine Love, Divine Truth and Divine Wisdom.

Say all of this aloud; then watch what happens inside. With any feelings that arise, consciously keep your breathing as deep and even as you can, and take your breath into the feeling. As you do this, the intensity will eventually die away, and one more emotional program will have lost its power over you. Allow any physical release to process in its own time, and if you find your body tightening remember to relax your jaw and breathe through your mouth.

OVERSENSITIVITY

The mental and emotional programs that your mortal mind runs can lock your energy right out of your center, and even out of your body. When the latter occurs you are living outside yourself. In normal circumstances this only comes about when some deep fear has been triggered, but it can persist for a long time. Its most obvious demonstration is when you are in shock.

The shock reaction is a natural body defense mechanism that closes down an injured part – withdraws energy and awareness from it – in order that the rest of the body can continue to function and survive. In emotional and psychological terms, the mind shuts down to give itself time to readjust to changes that impact the reality-construct it has based its identity upon. If these cannot be rationalized into a form that supports your self-identity the chances are that they will be buried deep and forgotten. They will be denied and ignored for ever more because allowing them into the light of day undermines the identity your mortal mind has created for itself.

Oversensitivity is a condition that reflects the presence of a higher than average degree of residual shock from the process of incarnation. It also indicates that the mind has remained more tuned in to the subtle realms than the physical and that you are operating more strongly through the *principle of interconnection*. A major contributor to the stress that you feel is the inability to function fully through the *principle of separation* in the same way as almost everyone else here.

The more sensitive you are from birth – that is to say the less your mind was tuned to this physical reality – the greater the likelihood that you will not be in your body. When you are outside your body you have difficulty connecting with the mundane physicality of everyday objects. In this condition the material world has little or no relevance, and this results in the exhibition of various levels of dysfunction. Some of the main symptoms of this are as follows:

- Lack of physical dexterity – the body never seems to comply with your need to control it.
- Bumping into things – physical objects are not recognized as being in the same space.
- Being prone to accidents – the world is full of dangerous objects that you don't see coming.
- Difficulty with mechanical devices and anything technical – technology seems to break down, particularly computers, printers and photocopiers.
- Emotional fragility – over-reaction to anything that seems to be going wrong.
- Absent-mindedness – difficulty holding anything relating to day-to-day existence in memory.
- Otherworldly focus – constantly distracted by psychic perception (visions, voices, sensations).
- Mental and emotional instability – inability to process the information received or distinguish between the various realities perceived.
- Difficulty being in crowds, cities and energy-dense places.
- Difficulty in opening up to people, and just being with people.
- Extreme difficulty with the brutality, pain, suffering and violence prevalent in the physical world.

When these symptoms are chronic, or persistent, it's an indication of severe ungroundedness. They nearly always go hand in hand with acute psychic abilities, even though these can go unrecognized. However this kind of ability stems from non-resonant tuning of the mind with this physical reality, rather than evolving from spiritual development. It's important to understand that there is nothing wrong with this kind of psychic ability in itself. It is indeed a gift, possibly one of the most demanding as it is excruciatingly painful and difficult to master and integrate.

If any of the above symptoms is particularly relevant to you, you might consider how you manage your sensitivity. I suggest you re-visit the chapter on sensitivity and work with the psychic protection procedures given there.

BRINGING YOUR ENERGY INTO YOUR BODY

You can bring your energy into your body and facilitate the onset of the witness state consciously by centering yourself as described earlier. The basic practice works extremely well, and is a practical tool that you can use anywhere. However if you have more space, time and privacy it can be augmented as follows. This is a training that will shift your entire relationship to the world over time. The basic practice then becomes a reinforcement for your mind and body.

Sit with your spine erect and both feet on the floor. Place your hands so that the fingertips of one touch the fingertips of the other one-for-one, including your thumbs. [In future this will be referred to as the *centering mudra*]. Close your eyes, and give your intent by saying aloud the sacred space formula...

> ➤ I {insert name in current use}, incarnated as {insert full birth name}, call to me the infinite resource of all that I am under **Universal Law**; and I now give intent that I remember and reclaim the sovereignty and integrity of my being and bodies as a Divine expression of **Universal Consciousness**. I call upon the **Essence of my Presence**, **my Guides** and **the Intelligence of Spirit** at the **Highest Level of the Light** to support and facilitate this process in me ... and I give thanks that this is so.

The next step is to take the three breaths. However instead of just drawing yourself inside your skin, you are to imagine that your entire energy field is being drawn inside you, into your center (*Tan Tien*). Breathe as deeply as you can, allowing your belly to expand on the in-breath and to shrink on the out-breath. After the third breath, sit quietly watching your breath in and out. If your mind starts to distract you, take the three breaths again. Get used to what it feels like to be fully in your center. Stay with this for as long as you can. There is no time stipulation. Anything you can do is good, and a half-hour is plenty.

PRACTICAL

Most physical activity will bring your energy into your body to some degree. The more you are absorbed in the activity, the more in your body you will be. To experience the effect of bringing your energy into your center here are three experiments you can try with a friend.

Stability

➤ Stand facing each other, just a little less than your arm's length apart. Have your backs straight and your feet a little apart. Then reach out and give your friend a gentle but firm push on the shoulder. Watch the effect. How stable is your friend? Was it necessary to regain any footing to maintain balance?
Then come back together, facing each other again. This time tell your friend to breathe into the belly, and imagine that s/he is completely centered there. Keep your friend's attention on that part of their body referencing the breath and the movement of the diaphragm. Then reach out and push gently at the shoulder again. How stable is your friend now? What is the difference? Swap over and try this for yourself.

Rooting

 ≈ Sit back to back on the floor with your legs out straight
in front of you and your hands resting on your thighs. Now,
pushing only with your feet by raising your knees, attempt
to push each other along the floor. The chances are that the
heavier of the pair of you will move the lighter.

 Resume your position sitting back to back, and before you
begin the pushing contest breathe into your center (do not
tell your companion about this). Also visualize roots growing
out of the base of your spine digging deep into the earth,
reaching through as many floors as necessary to do this. Hold
this visualization throughout the contest. It will be much
more difficult for anyone to move you in this condition. Quite
diminutive ladies can defeat substantial strong men in this
game.

Getting Heavy

 ≈ Stand relaxed with your feet together and your arms at your
sides. Get your companion to lift you bodily from the ground
– or get two companions to do this together. How easy is it
for them?

 Next, center yourself and breathe yourself into your belly
again. Imagine that all of your being is present inside your
skin, and keep bringing it in with your breath. (You can also
try rooting yourself through your feet.) Now ask your friend to
attempt to lift you again. Is there a difference?

8.

The Journey from Head to Heart

Your words would seem like wisdom but for the warning in my heart.

SPOKEN BY FRODO BAGGINS IN PETER JACKSON'S
FILM "THE FELLOWSHIP OF THE RING"
BASED ON J R R TOLKIEN'S NOVEL

SPIRITUAL INTELLIGENCE – THE PATH OF FEAR

Your *Spiritual Intelligence* is your innate guidance system. It is constantly seeking to inform you and guide you. It will never harm you. It will never lie to you. It is always there for you. It is the aspect of you that is universally wise. It is the greater part of you, the part that loves unconditionally. Yet if this is true, but I don't recognize or relate to anything I might regard as *Spiritual Intelligence*, the main question that arises logically is, *What do I have to do to connect with Spiritual Intelligence and hear what it is saying to me?*

There are many answers I could give to this question, but none of them would move you forward because it's the wrong question to ask. It's more a question of what you have to stop doing. And what you have to stop doing is ignoring yourself. You are spirit embodied, your wisdom is therefore that of *Spiritual Intelligence*. You are (I am) an integral expression of the great *Akashic Field of Universal Consciousness*. Your individual consciousness cannot be anything other than an aspect of the great continuum of Consciousness, which means the whole is present within you. The information carried in your being cannot be anything other than the wisdom of the universe – the *principle of universal wisdom*.

This statement is not a trite cop-out, but a truth to be embraced. So it needs to be expressed, even if at the moment you can't fully believe it. But if you can just be open to the possibility that some part of the statement is true you have taken the first step on the way to discovering the deeper truth for yourself – and that is exactly what you have to do.

> *I is 1*
> *and*
> *1 is ALL*

You can only discover *Spiritual Intelligence* for yourself. Nobody who discovers *Spiritual Intelligence* can tell anyone else exactly how to do it, or exactly what it is. We can be given descriptions, we can be shown someone else's way, and this is extremely valuable but only up to a point. Even though there will be considerable agreement with the way of another it will never be quite the same as your way. So there comes a moment when you have to take responsibility for your own wisdom. You have to take the risk that someone else will say you've got it wrong. Almost inevitably this will be the point that carries the most intense fear.

Spiritual Intelligence is not something you can learn intellectually, and it cannot be taught because you already know it. It's an intrinsic quality that has been concealed from you by your beliefs. Those beliefs have been created by the mortal mind in response to what it has decided about reality. Your beliefs both sustain and are sustained by your concept of the consensus reality that you exist within, and they ensure your compliance with it. This can all seem like a vast conspiracy to personally disempower the individual, but remember, if it is you are responsible for the perpetuation of it.

But if you cannot learn how to be spiritually intelligent, what you can learn is how to put yourself in situations where *Spiritual Intelligence* will reveal itself to you. This will take you out of the self-sabotaging conspiracy loop. However such a path is charged with fear because the situations you will be led into will challenge your concepts of reality and truth, and your self-identity.

> *Always be prepared to look at the world differently,*
> *it will change as you do.*

Many people begin this journey thinking that they will change their ways. They change jobs, home and relationships. Yet after a while they find that they are still living a routine that fails to give them the sense of meaning and fulfillment they were looking for. Many people get to a point of relative satisfaction and stop, because they come up against a situation that matches something they decided long ago they would not venture into. Many others stop almost as soon as they start, on seeing the potential upheaval the journey will create in their lives. The common thread through every incidence of frustrated or thwarted fulfillment is fear but this is seriously compounded by the ignorance of the mortal mind.

> *Ignorance is denial in its densest form.*
> *It is the wilful pretence of the mortal mind that*
> *there is no more to life*
> *than what it judges rational and sensible.*

For me, overcoming the particularly pernicious spiritual ignorance of the mortal mind has been as vital as walking through my fear. As I peel back the layers of ignorance I become increasingly aware that *Spiritual Intelligence* is the part of me that is pure truth. It's the higher intelligence that resides within me and moves through me, *in*-forming me all the time.

Spiritual Intelligence manifests itself through the inner voice that can be so difficult to hear, or easy to ignore, as it doesn't 'speak' in conventional ways. So I've had to learn to hear it and decode it, and I've had to learn to do this for myself, because the signature of my *Spiritual Intelligence* is unique to me. What isn't unique is the primary mechanism that disconnects me from this intelligence, but before I address that mechanism I need to say something about the subtle bodies.

THE SUBTLE BODIES AND THEIR RELATION TO THE PHYSICAL

The mental and emotional bodies form a part of our subtle energy make-up, and they extend out from the physical body as aspects of the aura. These subtle bodies are elements of what has been widely known as the astral body. There are many models for how they might be configured, and all of these have something to commend them. The differences mostly arise out of the attempt to express a multi-dimensional abstract concept through the resources of a mind tuned to earthly existence with all its reality prejudices and representational limitations.

As with the chakras, in the previous chapter, I'm going to adopt a simplistic model. This is one that sees the physical, emotional, mental and spiritual bodies fitting inside each other like Russian dolls. The physical body, as the densest is on the inside; then comes the emotional body. The next is the mental body, and then the spiritual body, which eventually merges with the *Universal Field of Consciousness*. The subtle bodies connect to the physical body in many ways, but most specifically at the seven main chakras. Remember none of this is how it is; it's simply a model to help the mortal mind out of its dilemma of having no reference points.

With the exception of the physical body, which is enclosed by the skin, none of these bodies is clearly defined with precise boundaries. They are not simply layered. They flow into each other spatially and dimensionally. This means that the subtle energy bodies permeate each other and, more important to understand, they permeate the physical body as well as progressively extending outwards from it. Any change in the disposition of one of the bodies is therefore reflected in each of the others. Because of this we can work on the subtle bodies, particularly the mental and emotional, and effect a change in the physical. We can also work on the physical and create a change in the subtle aspects.

Because of the overlap of all the bodies in the region bounded by the physical body, shifts in the expression of the subtle bodies are felt in the physical. The subtle presence of *Spiritual Intelligence* is therefore a felt sensation. This can be as spurious pain, twitches, twinges, tingling sensations, pressure sensations, tension, relaxation, inexplicable temperature changes, shivers – especially in the spine, and goose-bumps, amongst other phenomena.

It is the job of the mortal mind to find keys to understanding these symptoms and phenomena, and to find interpretations that affirm and support life. However, the mortal mind seldom figures this out because there is little cultural validity given to the process. In addition, over the course of history, there are only a few individuals who have managed to understand this sufficiently to embody their own presence with full consciousness. So there are not many people around who can tell us how to look within and what to look for.

More often than not when we have asked about odd sensations as children we have been told they are nothing and to forget about them. The consequence is that we learn to ignore our own *in*-formative sensing processes.

The same thing happens with dreams, visions and inner voices, but these are also often associated with insanity and the attendant horrors of the historical treatment of madness. In absolute terms the certification of someone as insane totally invalidates that person's life; it reduces her or him to living out a non-existence. This looks like annihilation to the observing (sane) mortal mind. So the mind is programmed with a strong cultural imperative to ignore any subtle sensations or unconventional imaginings.

Opening up to and connecting with the subtle realms and the intelligence of spirit may therefore be considered stupid and highly dangerous. As far as the mortal mind is concerned the consigning of subtle sensations and weird imaginings to oblivion is a vital survival strategy for the living organism it is identified with.

THE MECHANISM OF DISCONNECTION

Emotional reaction is the mechanism by which the mortal mind effects disconnection from *Spiritual Intelligence*. Emotional reaction is a function of my mental and emotional bodies which is felt through my physical body as the urge to flee, or even to turn and fight for my life. This is outlined in the *principle of reaction*.

The physical body's response to danger is to run away, or in extremes fight for survival. This is a primal (feeling) response of self-preservation, and it occurs in the physical body.

Anything that appears to threaten the notion of reality that I define myself around and participate with will trigger a fear reaction from my mind. Such a threat is effectively seen as a threat to my existence, as what I consider to be reality determines who I think I am. It therefore maps onto, and is associatively linked, with the fight or flight survival mechanism.

So, emotional reaction is the unconscious auto-defense response to an action or circumstance perceived by my mortal mind as a threat to my existence, or more accurately as a threat to the identity and reality it has constructed for me – *its* existence. This represents the ultimate danger, annihilation, which in physical terms equates to death.

My mortal mind's fear of annihilation induces phantoms of the physical body's primal responses through the subtle dynamic continuum of the mental and emotional bodies. My mind hi-jacks my feelings through the domain of emotions. This can cause me to feel responses to situations according to any dysfunctional psychological patterns and programs that my identity has been structured around. Such responses are **reactive** and they include defensiveness, resentment, anger, jealousy, guilt, shame, blame, judgment, criticism, aggression and deeply polarized behavior of all kinds. It is worth noting that polarized behavior includes relief, satisfaction, gratification and approval, which may well be considered positive and thus convince me that I have taken the right course of action.

When I feel any of this reactive emotion and act according to its imperative it overrides and disconnects me from the communication of *Spirit,* which also presents through my feelings. It distracts me from what is really going on, allowing the mind to continue as it was – in control.

My reaction is a device by means of which my mortal mind keeps my self-identity, and thus the mortal mind itself, secure. It does this under the pretence of keeping my physical being secure, as my mind also sees my physical body as the signifier of my/its existence. That is to say the material existence of the body is seen as the proof of the reality of the mind's constructs. Once this process is understood every reaction becomes a tool for personal growth, because it can be seen as a signal that some misinterpretation process is running the show.

THE UNCONSCIOUS BLOCKS

The unconscious blocks to the expression of *Spiritual Intelligence* manifest in the energy field. They can be felt as spurious sensations, as described above. Some people can see them, but be cautious about taking on someone else's interpretation of your experience. The *principle of projection* is always in operation. Blocks are also discernible as imbalances in the chakras. These are often perceived internally as the psychological trauma and issues we carry from our past and the fears we have for our future.

Very basically, for *Spiritual Intelligence* to express clearly from within the upper three chakras must be aligned with the heart. This implies a surrender of the intellect to the passion of the heart. However, it is a universal truth, one often overlooked, that the higher chakras can only function in direct relation to the conditions present in the lower three. The heart can only open to the degree that the lower three chakras are cleared. The expression of the throat is always prejudiced by what is held in the root, sacrum and solar plexus. The vision of the third eye reflects those values that are held in the lower three chakras and lived-out in daily life. The crown chakra tends to open in a way that matches any imbalance in the chakras below it, which in turn reflect the conditions in the subtle bodies.

What all of this boils down to is that the more the fears and trauma relating to the lower three chakras are cleaned up the more connected you will be with your heart, and the more clearly your *Spiritual Intelligence* will express. These issues of survival and physical vitality; sexuality, identity and creativity; power, control and ownership, (refer Chapter 7) are generally what people are most afraid of facing up to because of the mental anguish and 'heartache' that goes with them. Now is the time to begin befriending them because they are the signposts of your spiritual path and the keys to the evolution of your consciousness. Any heartache you feel is the pain of keeping your heart closed, NOT the pain of opening it!

For as long as these issues remain unresolved to they will constitute the blocks that disconnect you from *Spiritual Intelligence*. You experience the effects of a block every time you react to a person or a situation, every time you see something *wrong* with anyone else, every time you berate yourself for any shortcoming, every time you see yourself as a victim of circumstance, every time you compare yourself unfavorably with another ... and every time you pretend to yourself that you don't do these things. The list is endless.

You disconnect from yourself, and consequently *Spirit,* whenever you allow a situation to persist that fails to nourish you. Yet we all do it. Often although we may have come to terms intellectually with the circumstances of our lives a reaction can still be triggered from our cellular memory, or the ancestral memory. This is a complete mystery to the mortal mind because it thinks it has dealt with everything – especially if it has submitted to therapy and counseling procedures. This is one of the major areas where working with *Spiritual Intelligence* can bring about a deep transformation.

Christopher was born into a high-achieving academic family. He was dyslexic at a time when dyslexia was only barely becoming known about as a natural variation in the manifestation of the human form rather than a symptom of stupidity. So he found school excruciating. Despite working hard he had difficulty with all his written subjects. He was shamed and ridiculed by teachers, and browbeaten by his parents who couldn't hide their disappointment in their son. At last at the age of eighteen he finally failed the entrance examination for the elite university his family earmarked for him. This was a family disaster, the shame of which they might never recover from. Christopher went to a different 'second rate' college, and thrived.

What no-one had realized was that Christopher was very imaginative and creative, and he was very good with people. He was sensitive and empathic. His experience of being treated harshly when he had worked and worked to get good school results had given him a deep sense of compassion for anyone who was a bit slow. Christopher became hugely successful as a manager in a manufacturing business. He earned a high salary, was respected by all his staff and had a good marriage. By the time he had reached mid-life it seemed that he had come to terms with his early "failure" in life, but although he had achieved a lot he had a problem with his confidence. His career had plateaued and he was feeling very frustrated with his work because he knew he was capable of much more. He actually found himself working hard to try to impress his immediate boss, and failing again, repeating his earlier patterns. Eventually he found his way to me.

Once Christopher had talked about his background, it was fairly obvious that he was still carrying the residual trauma of his early shame and ridicule. We invoked *Spiritual Intelligence* to release the effects of this from his cells and from his mental and emotional bodies, and to re-integrate the energy that had been holding any compensatory behavior pattern for so many years. A few weeks later Christopher was responding much more firmly to any criticism from his own boss. He could see that the criticism came from his boss's insecurity and revealed more about his difficulties with life than Christopher's. Shortly after this Christopher was head-hunted for a very senior position in the company, one that fully acknowledged the unique contribution he had to make.

DISCERNMENT OF FEELING

One of the major difficulties facing all seekers after truth is that the emotions express as feeling. But *Spiritual Intelligence* resides in the body and also expresses through feeling. So if the emotional body is cluttered with the pain of the past – and the mental body is programmed to ensure that such pain and anguish are never experienced again – you will never hear what *Spirit* is truly saying to you. All you will ever do is create interpretations based upon your emotional and intellectual prejudices. This is your programming.

The emotional body is the most challenging of all the energy bodies to clear, because it feels so intense. We have learned to fear this intensity, so we devise strategies to control it with the mind. Some of us even teach ourselves not to feel in an attempt to convince ourselves that we have made it to a good space – this is called denial and it's very effective. These tactics take up a lot of our life-force energy.

Additionally, as long as the mind is allowed to charge the emotional body with fear, the mental body will continually replenish anything cleared emotionally. This creates a loop of continual processing. New blocks are created which cause scenarios based on fear, anger and control, to continue to be acted out, even though there might be a conscious effort to move away from these reactive patterns.

This cycle can develop into a kind of 'martyr syndrome'. People get so used to the process of emotional catharsis and adopt it as a part of their identity. They see themselves as committed to the healing process in ways that others are not. Their suffering is seen as the inevitable consequence of their service to the world, and worn as a badge of truth. This is clearly an issue that relates to both second and third chakras – elitism and significance, collaborative attributes forming a self-sustaining dysfunctional loop.

Sometimes blocks come from issues that are buried so deep it's hard to access their origins. But, inevitably, they are all issues that have come to be recognized as characterizing the lower chakras. We have learned to view these issues with distaste, excluding them from what is considered to be proper in society. Because of this they are loaded with stigma, shame and judgment, and that makes shifting them more difficult. They are often referred to as the *shadow*.

It is actually a natural function of *Spiritual Intelligence*, one we remain largely ignorant of, to clear the emotional body and the mental triggers that charge it. It is also a remarkably simple process, though not necessarily easy. The core of this process is to give intent and to dialogue aloud with whatever presents in you. This incorporates the power of sound – the sound of your own voice into the healing process.

This is extremely effective. If you are following the process of this book, rather than merely reading it at an intellectual level, you will have already had some experience in this. Be patient with yourself as you follow this path. You are working energetically. You are creating changes at a subtle level that will inevitably permeate into the physical level of your existence.

This will happen more quickly than you might imagine, but it may be less dramatic than you expect. The commonest outcome of this work is that people are unable to remember what it was that they got upset about, only noticing when something comes up that they used to react to and marveling that the reaction is gone. The other major effect is that the feeling of *Spiritual Intelligence* moving within becomes more discernible. The witness state is more and more readily accessed, which makes it easier to recognize your reactive patterns, and to be honest with yourself in relation to them. The process is organically progressive.

> *The key to recognizing if you are in reaction is blame.*
> *If you are seeking to blame someone else or some*
> *external situation for your feeling*
> *you can be certain that you are in reaction.*

EMOTIONAL CLEARING PRACTICAL

This section builds on the one in the last chapter. When you give intent to work with *Spiritual Intelligence,* you are actually giving permission for your soul consciousness to intervene in your physical existence. *Spirit* will give no assistance unless you do this. It may attempt to communicate with you in many ways, but it will not interfere in your life unless you ask. This is one of the meanings of Jeshua's words: "... ask and you shall receive, that your joy may be full" *(John 16:23-24).*

The *principle of alignment* (principle of free-will) means that *Spiritual Intelligence* can only operate through you by consent and invitation, irrespective of your conscious awareness or ignorance. Your personality ego – the false identity created by the mortal mind – will stay in control of your life, for as long as you accept it as your true identity. Having free will means having the freedom to refuse. This is the freedom to follow the willful false ego of the mortal mind, or to align with your soul – *Spiritual Intelligence.* Sooner or later the pain of resistance will be too great to bear on your own. How long that will be depends only on the level of your emotional pain threshold: until you say to yourself *there's got to be a better way* and really mean it.

The approach to clearing the emotions given in chapter seven invites *Spirit* to bring to our attention anything we need to address in order to bring us closer to the expression of our true selves. We then have to be present with any feelings that surface. This means allowing ourselves to feel without judging ourselves for what we are feeling, without wishing for the feeling to go away and without holding onto the feeling beyond its natural duration. When the feeling has exhausted itself the emotional body is clear. Allowing feelings to come out in this way forms the basis for clearing issues from the emotional body.

None of this sits easily with the rational mind, but if we stop the feeling for any reason or use a mental strategy to avoid it, we sabotage the process. The feeling can often be uncomfortable and this is why we may want to shut it down, but what you feel is what is leaving and the process can be facilitated by breathing deeply into any emotional feeling that appears. For most of us there is a lot of emotional healing to do. We've shut our feeling faculty down substantially, and held things in, in the mistaken belief that we ought to remain calm at all times and at any cost causing resentments to rage inside us..

There are three steps to this procedure for emotional healing. The first is to invite *Spirit* to work with you to clear anything that you are ready to release. This is done using a variation on the format given as EMOTIONAL CLEARING in the last chapter. This step is important because it surrenders control to your *Spiritual Intelligence*, so that you don't simply decide what's best for yourself out of thinking that you know what you need to do. As with all process protocols given in this book, center yourself first and then give your intent by speaking aloud.

> ➤ I {insert name in current use}, incarnated as {insert full birth name}, call to me the infinite resource of all that I am under **Universal Law**; and I now give intent that I remember and reclaim the sovereignty and integrity of my being and bodies as a Divine expression of **Universal Consciousness**. I call upon the **Essence of my Presence**, **my Guides** and **the Intelligence of Spirit** at the **Highest Level of the Light** to support and facilitate this process in me ...
>
> I invite any being or consciousness of the Light, who has experience and expertise in the areas relevant to me in this moment, to be with me working through me bringing guidance, direction and support. And I particularly ask the Consciousness of ... {insert the name of any guide(s) who you

relate to strongly}... for assistance with this.

And throughout this process I ask that the space I occupy, this room, be completely filled and surrounded with Divine Love, Divine Light, Divine Truth and Divine Wisdom.

Spirit, please work with me at every level: physical, emotional, mental and spiritual. Assist me now to transform and release the most appropriate layers of TRAUMA, FEAR-BASED CONDITIONING AND ASSOCIATED PROGRAMMING that I carry, which cause me to continue to identify with my mind, and which prevent me from embodying and expressing the truth of my being. Work especially with my mind, my mental body and my emotional body, and bring to my conscious awareness anything that is ready to leave, now.

Watch what happens inside. Watch for anything that flashes into your mind, any feelings that arise, or any sensation in the body. Consciously maintain your breathing as deep and even as you can. It's very easy, here, to move into ultra-shallow breathing as your mind's defense programs cut in to mask your feeling sense, and it is not at all unusual for the energy to come right out of the body leaving it without feeling and vitality in a miasma of deadness. But practice and perseverance will pay dividends.

The mortal mind can be particularly elusive here, something may come fleetingly which you will tell yourself is irrelevant, just as quickly. If this happens know that the fleeting thought or image is what you're after, even if it makes no sense. Staying present with this eventually brings clarity. It's like telling your mind that you've spotted something and you're not going to let it get away with hiding it from you again.

Also you can easily be fooled into thinking that nothing is happening when your body is producing subtle sensations, as you've become so used to regarding these as nothing. So pay attention! Sometimes there will be obvious pain. Anything that arises is a key that *Spirit* is communicating to you through the medium of your body.

The next step is to bring whatever has arisen to a crisis. This is the same principle as the idea of a physical healing crisis. If the crisis is not reached some residue of disease will remain. This is rather like ensuring an abscess or boil is fully ripe before lancing it. So you must be prepared to endure some discomfort, this is usually relatively brief. It is always much less than you fear it will be.

The procedure is simply to ask *Spirit* to intensify the condition that has come to mind, and show you what lies underneath at the root of it. As before, you do this by speaking your intent aloud according to the structure given below.

> ~ Spirit, please intensify the tension, pain, feeling ...
> [describe what has come up, and where it's located in you body if that's relevant] ... Suffuse it with Love, and release it. And show me what's underneath at the root of this now!

At this point some clarity around what has come up will be received. Often there will be some childhood experience – emotional upset, humiliation, bullying, abuse etc. – come to mind. Sometimes there will be an unresolved relationship experience. These are the most common, but anything can come to light. And there may also be some emotional intensity. Take your breath into this, as described earlier. As you do this, the intensity will eventually die away, and the reaction to whatever traumatic experience surfaced will fade with it. Allow any physical release to process in its own time, and if you find your body tightening remember to relax your jaw and breathe through your mouth.

The beauty of working with *Spirit* in this way is that you are never given anything that you are not ready for or competent to deal with. So if you practice regularly with these techniques *Spirit* will teach you the subtleties of the energy as you go. You will also come across many inspirational ideas for how you can work with *Spirit* to deepen the process.

The final step is to ask for all the tension trauma and attendant programming that the situation, or event, created in you to be melted away. Again this is done through your spoken intent, remembering that your entire cellular structure responds to the sound vibration of your voice.

⪼ Spirit, please go deep into my cellular memory and melt away all the tension and trauma that the experience of this situation/these events ... [name them specifically, and anyone involved] ... created in me. Erase all the defense structures and programming I created in reaction to this and replace everything with Divine Love, Divine Light, Divine Truth and Divine Wisdom now! And I give thanks that this is so.

When this is done you should allow some time to for your energy to settle. This kind of emotional work goes to the deepest levels. Sensitivity to your own process is essential. It is not a good idea to create a shopping list of all the issues you know you must have and work through it mechanically. This is simply a trick of the mortal mind trying to prove that it's got the message of being conscious. However, if you already know from a recent reactive experience what the issue you want to clear is, this procedure can be adapted as follows:

⪼ I {insert name in current use}, incarnated as {insert full birth name}, call to me the infinite resource of all that I am under **Universal Law**; and I now give intent that I remember and reclaim the sovereignty and integrity of my being and bodies as a Divine expression of **Universal Consciousness**. I call upon the **Essence of my Presence**, **my Guides** and **the Intelligence of Spirit** at the **Highest Level of the Light** to support and facilitate this process in me ... and I give thanks that this is so.

I invite any being or consciousness of the Light, who has experience and expertise in the areas relevant to me in this moment, to be with me working through me bringing guidance, direction and support. And I particularly ask the Consciousness of ... [insert the name of any guide(s) who you relate to strongly] for assistance with this.

And throughout this process I ask that the space I occupy, this room, be completely filled and surrounded with Divine Love, Divine Light, Divine Truth and Divine Wisdom.

Spirit, please work with me at every level: physical, emotional, mental and spiritual. Go deep into my cellular memory and melt away all the tension and trauma I carry in relation to ...
< Here you insert the details of the issue/incident that you have become aware of.>
... Work with my mind, my mental body and my emotional body and erase all the defense structures and programming I created in reaction to this ... Dissolve any mind-set, thought-form or mental body strategy that sustains the trauma pattern in me ... Replace everything with Divine Love, Divine Light, Divine Truth and Divine Wisdom now!
... And I give thanks that this is so.

Working in this way with yourself is very empowering as it brings the gift of self-trust. So many teachers promise empowerment yet insist that you surrender your power to them and adopt their prejudices. The leader's perspective, and any associated dysfunction, has to be supported even if it conflicts with what you feel to be true for yourself. By aligning with your own *Spiritual Intelligence*, you put a stop to the self-invalidation that ensues from giving preference to someone else's interpretation of your situation. Your full potential as a human being is then free to emerge. Do also remember, however, that there is much to be learned by submitting to a teacher's prejudices as they do help you to develop clarity about the way you want your truth to express.

RAISING YOUR LEVEL OF CONSCIOUSNESS

The long-term effects of clearing your emotional body in this way are profound. There can be physiological changes as well as psychological shifts. In spiritual terms your heart will begin to open without any effort from you. This opening will continue to widen, and it will draw more of your *Spirit* into your body. This means your crown chakra will open wider, your third-eye will become more perceptive and your vocal expression will become more heart centered. You will also find that you become more conscientious in everything you do, your levels of authenticity and integrity will rise. You will become more conscious.

This effect of an opening in the upper chakras being produced as a consequence of de-toxing your lower three chakras is a reversal of many other spiritual practices which focus on opening the upper chakras to connect with *Spirit*. However there is no conflict here. This does not make other practices wrong. *Spiritual Intelligence* walks a two-way street. Everything has its value. However, it is to be remembered that bringing more energy in through the crown will always require a corresponding 'detox' of lower chakra issues.

This means that whenever you attempt to progress spiritually by working with your upper chakras there will be an inevitable emotional fall-out in the lower three. Sometimes the fall-out can be very intense and last for weeks, months or even years. This is because the rest of the body takes time to catch up with and acclimatize to the new levels of energy it is holding. If the fall-out is ignored higher level energies cannot be grounded and integrated. When this happens you will not be fully present in your body. In some cases, where there are high levels of resistance to the emotional clearing process, the effect can be that the person concerned ends up living completely outside themselves. They are out of their body.

The chaos this produces is a familiar phenomenon to many on a path of spirituality. But chaos is not a necessary adjunct to spiritual growth. It is NOT 'meant to be'. It can be avoided by staying present in your body, and consciously engaging with your emotional clearing. The more grounded you can be with all spiritual energies, the more energy you will bring through. This is a natural consequence of spiritual growth.

> True intelligence is the capacity of the mind to
> yield to the wisdom of the heart.
> Have the courage to act as you feel you must in
> spite of what you think.

EGO SHATTERING

One of the primary effects of consistent work with *Spiritual Intelligence* is what I call ego shattering. This is the collapse of the false ego created by the mortal mind. It is a curious phenomenon that relates to what is often called the old male paradigm, and it is something that men find more difficult than women to encounter. It is characterized by a feeling of total mental and emotional confusion.

Much of the mortal mind's self identity is structured around doing what is right, the *principle of approval*. This can be thought of as what is necessary in order to be considered a good man or woman, or perhaps what is necessary in order to be a *real* man or woman. However as the mind begins to see through its own artifice and the artifice of the conventions it has sought to appease it is faced with the conundrum of what to do to be sure of getting things right. It is unable to make a decision based on any firm data and all of its critical and polemic voices start to speak at once. The experience is bordering on the psychotic and very uncomfortable. But this is the point of surrender where the mortal mind begins to come into alignment with the *Essence* of your being.

At the crisis the experience is nearly always accompanied by uncontrollable and convulsive weeping as the mental/emotional energy structures in the astral body are dissolved. It's as if the mind is apologizing to the soul for being so crass. In the aftermath of this there is a freshness about you. One way to describe it would be as a return to innocence, where the suspicions and cynicism based on experience give way to openness, curiosity and allowing. Many old defensive strategies are swept away. They are now redundant as your own presence takes on the duty of your protection.

THE DARK NIGHT OF THE SOUL

All who engage in the quest for their own truth experience the dark night of the soul. This can take many outward forms, but inwardly it is characterized by one thing, a sense of utter despair that nothing is working. Some of the ways this presents are listed below.

- Feeling and believing that everything you think and do is futile.
- Seeing your entire life as utterly pointless.
- Recognizing that you have done everything you possibly can in life the wrong way.
- Feeling utterly lost.
- Seeing no way forward for yourself.
- Feeling totally, desolately, alone.
- Lying awake with a desperate heartache all night.
- Lying awake with intense mental anguish all night.
- Weariness that saturates your mind, emotions and physical body.
- Acknowledging that coping with life is not living it.
- Contemplating your own death as all that's left to you.

The mortal mind is in meltdown at these times, and they are characterized by intense incapacitating feelings of fear. The artifice of the life the mind constructed for you is clearly seen for what it is, founded on misdirections, misinterpretations and the expediency of conventions. This is a conflict that is impossible for the mortal mind to cope with and the physical body is saturated with the mind's fear of annihilation that moves through the emotional and mental bodies.

The mortal mind will defend itself to the utmost in this process, at almost any cost to the body (or body of affairs). It firmly believes in its own integrity and ideals. Any suggestion that its ideals are misplaced has to be rationalized away if the mind's self-identity is to survive. It is only when the futility of this is fully *felt*, when it is clear that its entire self-identity structure is delusional and a perversion of the life force, that the mind will admit to knowing nothing. In this moment it gives up its control. This will seem like a total emotional and nervous breakdown; in clinical terms it may be, but in spiritual terms it is a breakthrough.

The mind can easily go into a self-critical backlash and wallow in thoughts and feelings of uselessness with this. If it does, look out for it. Know that all criticism is toxic, and invalid. The mind did the best it could with what was available to it at the time, even if it did know that it was conspiring in a lie. Know if this hadn't happened you would not be at the point of the evolution in your consciousness that you've now reached. Know that whenever you experience the dark night of the soul – and the chances are you will experience it more than once – it is a clear sign that you are on the right track. Ask *Spirit* for help with it!

A LITTLE BIT MORE ON CENTERING

Over the years I've been working with the form of giving intent and dialoguing given here, I have noticed a shift in my own centering process. I still use my breath to bring my energy into my center, but I've discovered that when my energy is centered in my heart it expands and extends to include my *Tan Tien*. So I now make it my practice to focus on my heart when I want to bring my energy into the center of my being. You may discover something else works better for you, as you become more self-aware. Whatever this is will be right for you, regardless of what anyone else tries to teach you. However, while you are learning about this I encourage you to continue to bring your energy into your *Tan Tien*. When you are ready to make a change *Spirit* will let you know – you will be unable to ignore it.

9.
Common Obstacles

*One word frees us of all the weight and
pain of life: That word is love.*

SOPHOCLES (496BC – 406BC)

The journey from head to heart is one that all seekers on the path must commit to. It is never a direct route, and each person's route is unique. So no-one can tell you what turns you will have to take. As you make this journey you will inevitably be presented with many obstacles on the path. Whatever the reality may seem to be, all of these will be of your own making. This is true for everyone on the journey, yet it is amazing how many of us devote a huge effort to trying to avoid facing these obstacles.

This chapter is a practical guide to identifying and eliminating common obstacles and their effects. Some of these obstacles, although common are nevertheless somewhat obscure when viewed from a conventional perspective. It is worth remembering that a conventional perspective is a serious obstacle to your self-empowerment. The *principle of creation and manifestation* operates in such a way that all influencing factors are accounted for, especially those we are not conscious of and those we want to deny.

If you haven't already realized it, the biggest obstacle to your self-empowerment through *Spiritual Intelligence* is you, or what you have learned to call *you*. This *you* is the false self-identity of the mortal mind and all the support structures the mind has allied (a-lied) with to construct the rationale for its existence.

When you are ready to let go of these structures they will begin to reveal themselves to you. This can happen in almost any fashion, but the result is always the same: some aspect of your life will stop working. Then, no matter how elaborately you try to create a new strategy so that you can carry on as before, you will somehow find yourself back at your unhappy starting point. You will go round and round in loops that will all seem different and new at first but will eventually turn into the same frustration.

These loops sometimes take years to spot, and all the time your life is passing. If they are seen and interpreted without a spiritually intelligent perspective they seed cynicism, world-weariness and depression. Most often this manifests in dead relationships and dead-end jobs, and it seems that most of us need to have our share before we determine to do something about the situation.

The good news is that nothing is as it seems. Once we realize that the dead relationship or job is a reflection of an inner deadness, and take responsibility for it we have taken the first step in reclaiming our own power. This is perhaps the most difficult because it's here that we have to open up to the fact that there is no-one else we can really blame for any predicament we find ourselves in. And if we start blaming ourselves we create another problem. The solution to this is to see ourselves as learners, rather than culprits, explorers rather than perpetrators.

RELATIONSHIPS AND EMOTIONAL TIE-CUTTING

It could be said that all human life is about relationships in some form or another. It can also be said that all relationships are an energy exchange of one form or another. This exchange needs to be balanced for it to be healthy. It also needs to be clean, by which I mean it needs to be free of agendas, assumptions and expectations, which is seldom the case.

The consequences of our "dirty" relationships are that we harbor grudges and hold on to old grievances. We leave a piece of our attention, our energy, in a troublesome incident long after the incident is past or the relationship has moved on or even after it is over. Sometimes we manage to rationalize the incidents which gave us grief, and convince ourselves that we are over them, but until we clear the emotional energy charge associated with them we are still under their influence.

The cutting of emotional ties is one of the fundamental processes in reclaiming our independence, the integrity of our autonomy – our personal sovereignty. It is often the single most important step in cleaning up relationships with other people.

There is always an interchange of energies at subtle levels when we connect with another person. These energies are loaded with our programs and agendas, control and expectations, judgment and criticisms. This is greatly amplified if there is any sexual content. Sometimes we take on these agendas consciously, that is we recognize the behavior of the other person as being out of alignment with where we are at but make a connection anyway. At other times the interchange is entirely unconscious. The tendency is for residues of old connections to contaminate future relationships, and to set limits on how we allow new relationships to manifest.

In a facilitator training group I lead one of the participants recently explained this self-limiting phenomenon in the following way:

> ≋ When you first meet me you see me closest to the way I really am. The next time you meet me you see an adapted me, where I have adapted to what I think you expect of me. Further meetings produce further adaptations. The same is true for you, so neither of us is relating from a place of authenticity.

> Neither of us knows what the other is really like, and we're both afraid to show each other our authentic selves.

What happens in the established consensus routine for interpersonal relating is that we interact on the basis of the conflict or agreement between our individual unconscious personal programming. Any deviation from expected behavior is deemed threatening and produces a reaction – fear, anger, judgment, disapproval etc. So until we make a decision to do something differently with our relationships they cannot be founded on conscious interaction and growth. Cutting the emotional ties is a major step towards conscious relating.

The purpose of tie-cutting is to clean up the dynamics of a relationship so it can express in its optimum, or highest form. This means letting go of our preconceptions of how things are supposed to be. When we cut the energy ties in relationships we are always working on ourselves and leaving anyone else involved free to make their own choices.

What this means at a personal level is that the more emotional investment I have in the outcome of an interaction the less integrity I will have with myself in the relationship. Consequently I will be potentially more disposed to sacrifice my self for the sake of a result that I consider to be favorable.

What is favorable can be anything, but it generally turns out to be what will elicit the approval of another and thus support my approval of myself. It does not matter what that favorable result is, but the more I have identified with what I consider to be favorable the less aligned with my true essence I become. The inner stress of this turns into depression and self-hatred, and will play itself out through *the principle of separation*.

In this context, another subtlety to watch out for is the way my self-interest will hide itself behind truth. This is the self-interest of my mortal mind. For it is also the case that if what I consider to be favorable does happen to align with my inner essence, but my motivation for any action has been to produce the favorable outcome rather than to respect my inner self, then I am still presenting myself in a condition of self-rejection. This is because I have only honored myself by accident, rather than by conscious intent. Such serendipity is easily misrecognised as "what was meant to be" and I can be all too ready to let myself off the hook by assuming this attitude.

The relative polarization of 'good' and 'bad' is foreshadowed here. In this context what is 'good' and what is 'bad' is only grounded in what I have learned and experienced through the filters of approval and acceptance. What is 'good' for one may be 'bad' for another, but that is completely irrelevant to my need for acceptance and my fear of rejection. If it happens that what I have identified as 'good' for me is 'bad' for another, my tendency will be to judge the other who holds the differing perspective as being 'bad'. However this can also work the other way and lead me to where I only see myself as bad in comparison to those who live more apparently virtuous lives.

This is all mortal-mind garbage. It is a psychology that underwrites almost every aspect of human interaction. It is underneath the blight of poor self-esteem that is fostered by consumerism and exploited through most commercial advertising. And it underpins all co-dependent relationships, which are sustained through the emotional blackmail of guilt, envy, shame, blame and humiliation.

At all times the principal guide through this minefield is the heart. The subtle feeling (sometimes not so subtle) of closing down, that the mind will want to override, is the surest sign that we are going against our true selves. This feeling is known to us all. It comes as a tightening, an inner shrinking, a stuck feeling or a constriction within the chest cavity. It has no rational attributes. In extreme cases there can be pain and physical reaction – coughing, choking, sneezing, shuddering, retching. It is important to develop your own methods for interpreting this feeling, and it is vital that you honor it.

IMPLICIT CONDITIONS, VALUES AND BELIEFS

There is little to be said about explicit conditions in relationships. These are generally articulated at some point, and we are able to choose to comply or accept the consequences of non-compliance. Whether the conditions are appropriate, or good, or bad is irrelevant, as long as they are explicit I am empowered. I know where I stand and I can choose my response. This is an energetically clean relationship structure, in that the boundaries are clear.

Complying with explicit conditions can still involve serious repression, which will ultimately create damage, but it is the effort to comply with implicit conditions that causes deep levels of distress. For a start, in personal terms I can never be quite sure what these conditions are so I cannot gauge my response in a way that ensures approval. Therefore if I am concerned with receiving approval, implicit conditions, values and beliefs inherently destabilize me and undermine my confidence. They carry the shadow of the fear that I will be rejected.

What most of us do to avoid this situation is develop defensive patterns of behavior designed to keep us safe from the consequences of getting it 'wrong'. Wrong in this context is simply behaving (or being seen to behave) in any way that brings disapproval and rejection. We adopt the *principle of separation* as our principal mode of existence. We create boundaries beyond which we will not allow ourselves to tread, such boundaries are generally well within what we consider to be propriety. We put ourselves in a straitjacket.

But what is more, we not only put ourselves in a straitjacket, we forget why we've done it and how we've done it. We read the unconscious energies present in our environment all the time and we see that everyone else is locked into their own straitjacket so it seems natural for us to be in our own. It is an aspect of earthly existence that we accept because no other alternative is offered or apparent. All this restriction then fades into a background routine we adopt as basic to survival. It feels normal, but it is nothing more than a habit. It is effectively a subliminal form of cultural institutionalization, which is all the more insidious because of its apparent transparency. The question to ask yourself is this: *Is this how I want to live?*

Other questions that will take you into this area of self-exploration are:

Who am I protecting from the truth about me?
Who am I protecting from themselves?
Who am I furious with, but dare not let them know?
Who am I carrying?
Whose anger and disapproval do I fear?
What is there about me that I must ensure nobody ever finds out?
What are the qualities in me that am I afraid to consider?

When I cut emotional ties with another, what I am intending is to reclaim the energies that I have projected onto the other and onto our relationship. My intent is to free myself from everything that keeps me tied into my straitjacket and to allow anyone else involved the freedom to cast off theirs. However, I take great care to make no demands that they do as that is simply an effort at control and a further projection of my judgement. Typical qualities and conditions that we take on (or introject), and project onto others are:

Personal Emotions: fear, anger, despair, resentment, jealousy, envy, guilt, shame, desire, greed, worry, grief ...
Inherited (and Learned) Behavior Patterns: control, humiliation, undermining, duty, abuse, violence, aggression, passivity, resignation, criticism, victimhood, self-denial, stigma, bitterness, suspiciousness, spite, cynicism ...
Unconscious Behavior Patterns: denial, self-rejection, expectation, prejudice, judgment, mistrust ...

These patterns are all interlinked, and there are many more. They can all inform the implicit conditions, values and beliefs that we seek to comply with, or that we insist upon compliance with, in our relationships. Individual relationships will demonstrate an infinite variety of combinations and self-sustaining energy loops that keep all participants disempowered and unconsciously complicit. A practical process for cutting these emotional energy ties and circuits, and for transmuting and reintegrating any dysfunctional aspects is given at the end of this chapter.

CORE IMPRINTING

Imprints are what cause us to think, feel, believe and behave 'as if', that is according to certain prescribed formulae. Core imprints can be considered as unconscious information configurations that we use as the criteria for our choice of action. They are not necessarily what drives us, but signposts to the road we (must) drive on. They incorporate the fundamental fears that underwrite our relationship with the world we live in. And we all have these, although we manifest and accommodate them differently, according to our individual circumstances and disposition.

At the most basic level core imprints relate to survival and procreation. These include the primal fears of death, extinction, starvation and predation, and the imperatives to breed and feed. These are carried in our cellular memories from our connection with all animal life. They are ingrained in us at the deepest physical level and can be considered to be hard-wired. This means they are virtually impossible to change, but we can learn to recognize them consciously and modify our behavioral responses.

Moreover we can learn to trust our hearts to lead us away from situations where our survival is threatened and our primal responses are triggered. We can also learn to trust that, if we find ourselves in such situations after listening to our hearts, we are there for a reason and there will be a major gift in the experience.

At another level core imprints concern the particular challenges, set up by the Soul, to be explored during a lifetime. Some traditions would refer to this as *karma*; when the karma is played out, or balanced the soul leaves and the body dies. There is a fatalistic quality to this perspective that defeats any aspiration to self-empowerment or self-realization. However, if we accept that it is possible to embody our own essence to a degree where we become self-realized then there may be a point where commitment to the spiritual path becomes the overwhelming priority. Such a point offers the Soul the potential to exceed what might have been planned, or to go beyond its karmic schedule.

Once this point is reached the relevance of the core imprints may well have been superseded, but the imprints themselves can still have a holding effect. We may have actually made it through the primary challenge of our lives with an appropriate degree of understanding and sensibility, yet the subtle process that locks the challenge (karma) in place remains active.

The imprints of these (karmic) challenges will continue to manifest as blocks to our expression, until we find some way to address them. They make themselves known by their persistence even after any emotional charge has been cleared, manifesting abject despair. Once they are known about, when they recur they become a major signal that action is needed.

Intellectual awareness is seldom sufficient to clear these blocks, although many coping strategies will give the appearance that they have been overcome. The most powerful of these strategies actually work to disconnect us from the feelings that the blocks produce. We can then go past any sticking place by using our minds and will, but the underlying tensions remain in our energy field.

ANCESTRAL IMPRINTING

Just like us, our ancestors also had core imprints, some coming from genetic origins, some from unfulfilled soul purposes and some originating in the trauma of their lives. Whatever our ancestors were unable to transcend and heal in themselves, they passed down to us in some way. This could be psychologically through mental strategies, energetically through feelings and emotions or even genetically through our cellular memory.

We may not even know what experiences created our ancestors' trauma, but we can still carry the scars of wounds that are older than we are, and our only clue to their existence is the areas of life that seem closed to us. We carry these scars subliminally, yet just opening up to the possibility that this is the case brings the potential to clear anything that we carry in this respect.

Like our core imprinting, our ancestral imprinting will also create obstacles to our expression, and understanding of ourselves.

Furthermore, we can pass this imprinting on to our children, in our turn, until we become aware of it and address it.

The following list is an indication of the kind of imprinting we can carry through our ancestral lineage. Remember that this potentially extends back to the origins of life ...

- the primal fear of death
- the primal fear of starvation
- the primal fear of predation
- the primal imperative to breed (mate and multiply no matter the cost to the body), which engenders the sexual imperative to violate, possess and control for personal gratification
- the imperative of competitiveness, which engenders the mental imperative to force my body to submit to the control and will of my mind
- the imperative to feed/fatten-up
- the fear of being discovered (seen/heard/sensed)
- the core fear of annihilation
- the core fear of abandonment
- the core fear of loneliness and isolation
- the core fear of pain, physical and mental illness
- the core fear of surrender, mistrust and betrayal and the imperative to control
- the core fear of childbirth, child-bearing, child-rearing, widow-hood
- the core fear of worthlessness ... that I am less than ... that there is something wrong with me
- a belief in struggle and hardship ... that life is tough
- poverty consciousness ... that wealth, affluence and prosperity pass me by ... that spending money is a luxury for others to enjoy
- powerlessness ... that I have no control over my destiny
- victim consciousness ... that if everything were different (or if others were different) I would be different
- the imprint of aggression, violence and abuse
- incest, sexual abuse and exploitation
- dependency and addiction (this can include a history of alcoholism)
- depression

- suicide
- murder, assassination, extermination and genocide
- crime and criminalization

All of these are potential aspects of traumatization that can be carried in the body. They are particularly insidious as they are held tightly in place by lies, deceit, secrecy, subterfuge, treachery, humiliation, shame and stigma. In addition they underpin cultural imprinting so much that in practical terms it is difficult to separate ancestral from cultural, the two are almost inextricably intertwined. However when individual core issues surface it is often clear where the originating trauma lies and what has kept it hidden and held it in place.

CULTURAL IMPRINTING

We all have a cultural identity of some kind. We look to it to justify our beliefs about right and wrong. It defines our ethical codes, our moral codes, our convictions, our working practices, our spiritual practice, and just about every aspect of our social order. And we take refuge in the sense of belonging that we derive from it. So we often perceive it as a nurturing agency, as an authority by which our own existence is validated, or as a surrogate for our wider spiritual family. This means we can be very attached to it, and very afraid to challenge it let alone surrender it. We are in fact surrendered *to* it before we get here.

The imprint of our cultural identity is inherent in our birth, and the way we are raised as children. It is determined in the geographical location of our arrival on the planet, and in the already established interaction with it of our progenitors – mum and dad. It predates us, and inescapably defines us before we even arrive. Some of it is indeed useful; it gives us reference points against which to establish a sense of who we might be. Through the *principle of self-identity* we make the assumption that this is who we are. We perceive our cultural identity as sustaining us, and in turn we sustain it through our belief in it.

Our cultural imprints structure the way we interpret ourselves and the world around us. Without them we face feeling the terrors of isolation and non-existence. But this can only happen because we have forgotten our connection to source. We have forgotten who we are and we allow the imprints to tell us. On the back of this ride all the mental and intellectual strategies we use to control and manipulate the feelings of loss and the other emotions our sense of disconnection engenders. Such strategies include philosophy, theology, ideology and psychology, politics, science and religion.

Cultural imprints set limits of approval. They establish a range within which we can permit ourselves to express, and within which we are permitted to express. They also govern our attitudes, and set the criteria by which we judge others and make decisions. Our cultural imprints specify who our friends are, and who are our enemies. They prescribe our principles of truth. They delimit our definition of what constitutes humanity which polarizes our view of what is inhumanity; who is human and who is **inhuman**; who deserves to live, and who deserves to die. This can force us to deny the existence of those parts within ourselves that do not qualify.

> *Our cultural imprints are collective mental body*
> *formulations for coping with the irrational – our*
> *core fears, core imprints and ancestral imprints.*

The qualities that define inhumanity are obscured by shame and stigma within the collective self-identity of the group which we see as giving us meaningful existence. Any inhuman qualities can now only exist outside our group, by definition. Any group that can be construed as differing from ours can be perceived as potentially inhuman. They may then be constructed as our enemies and earmarked for destruction.

Maintaining the integrity of our *humanity* (our idealized cultural concept of ourselves) engenders an imperative to eradicate *inhumanity*. Thereby, most of the violence and conflict we see expressed in the world receives justification. This is civilization. What we don't dare to think true of ourselves, we imagine is true of others. This is how one lot of humans *projects* their **inhumanity** onto another lot. Yet if we can **think** it, it's in us – a part of us which we are constrained to deny on pain of being ostracized.

An essential characteristic of our social and cultural systematization is that it purports to reduce our vulnerability, and increase our chances of survival. So our cultural imprinting rides on our core imprinting, the former often seeking to control or modify the latter. However, once the core imprinting has been recognized and tackled, much of the cultural imprinting becomes redundant. Yet it still resides within us supervising our interaction with the world, and it carries the weight of our ancestral imprinting, from generations upon generations of our ancestors.

At a soul level, of course we are not victims of this, but volunteers who have agreed to the experience. It is all relative to the particular form of separation from Spirit we have chosen to engage with and transform through the incarnation cycle. This element of transformation is an essential aspect of our service on planet Earth. Each one of us walking the planet contributes to the overall planetary consciousness. Correspondingly, we each *carry* a part of this consciousness, and it comprises all the various aspects of fear, conflict and prejudice that we seek to be free of. We actually modify the planetary consciousness when we change our own.

By choosing, and giving intent, to shift our consciousness we choose to connect with the particular elements of our own separation experience, at the deepest unconscious levels. This not only liberates us from the tyranny of our social imperatives – what other people think of us, and what we think of ourselves – it enables us to walk through our life challenges, our karma – and come out the other side, free.

CULTURAL IMPRINT IMPERATIVES

Our cultural imprints can be regarded as charging us with certain imperatives, beliefs and values that we must live by in order to fit into our society and justify our existence. Some of these are listed below:

- The imperative to express my being exclusively through the constraints of a consensus paradigm.
- The imperative to reject, dismiss and disparage every perspective other than the consensus paradigm as ignorance, nonsense, madness/insanity, weird, dangerous or wrong.
- The belief that anyone or anything OTHER than me [or OTHER than the mainstream cultural paradigm that I embody] is my enemy.
- The imperative to disable, maim, kill and destroy my enemies.
- The belief that my wounds can be assuaged or balanced by revenge, retaliation or retribution.
- The imperative to conform to stereotypes of gender, femininity and motherhood, masculinity and fatherhood, childhood.
- The duty to sacrifice my integrity to a consensus lie in order to participate in a stratified class or caste system or in any form of elitism ... particularly in respect of monarchy, and aristocracy, nationalism, patriotism and military service, religion or any hierarchical systematization of spiritual belief, esoteric societies (freemasons; hermetic orders, fraternities, exclusive cults or sects), the learned professions (law, medicine, accountancy, etc.), affluence and income, capitalism, business competition, occupation, property ownership, social status and influence ... patriarchy, matriarchy, feminism, chauvinism, sexism, homophobia, race, tribe (or skin color), age ... education, (school-system, scholastic achievement), academia or intellectualism ...

Extensive though it is, this is not meant to be an exhaustive list, nor is it hierarchical in any way. It is included to illustrate the variety of cultural programming we can inflict upon ourselves. And it is to be observed that many of these conditions map on to each other in allegorical, or archetypal, ways.

There are undoubtedly many delights and advantages embodied in cultural practices. It is where these mutate into coercive control structures that they transform into licenses for subjugation. Compliance then ensures self-violation, resentment, trauma and shame.

VOWS

Under this heading I include promises, contracts, agreements, decisions and all terminology that represents the taking of sworn decisions or confirmed statements that have a determining effect on the way we permit ourselves to express. This is effectively a process of self-suppression; it can be very unconscious and relentless in its effect. In the format that appears in the practical section at the end of the chapter I also use the terms covenants and oaths. These are archaic English terms which are nevertheless still in use in legal terminology, and can therefore still have a relevance. Any translation of this into other languages should take cognizance of this.

All vows are ultimately promises of some kind, and although they might appear to be promises to other people or external agencies they are really agreements with ourselves. For instance, if I promise that I will meet someone at a particular place and time I am also making an agreement with myself. The agreement with myself is to the effect that I will let go of anything that gets in the way of me keeping the promise to the other person. I am potentially prioritizing against myself in favor of someone else.

Everyday agreements of this kind are an essential part of our social fabric. Mostly they are insignificant in the general scheme of things, unless they are part of a habitual pattern of self-sacrifice. But the fact that these occurrences are largely insignificant easily overlooks those that are symptomatic of unhealthy behavior patterns.

Many unhealthy behavior patterns actually structure our everyday relationships. Yet because they are part of a social convention we fail to notice them, or if they are noticed they are rationalized as necessary in order to be able to interact with other people.

There are many vows that we take quite consciously, fully believing in their relevance to our lives. These include oaths of allegiance, vows of enmity and marriage vows. At the time we take these vows they will seem solemn and serious, which is an indication of the power we endow them with. They can all become redundant as we move through life, particularly as our consciousness shifts. Yet the energy we invested in these vows will be lost to us until we reclaim it in some way, and all the time it remains structured by the vow it has the potential to sabotage our self-expression.

Other vows are made in the form of personal decisions based on particularly pleasant or unpleasant experiences. Whenever we have a difficult experience and say to ourselves *I'm NEVER going to do that again* we imprint ourselves with a vow. The same thing happens if we say *I'm ALWAYS going to ...-...-...-...-... in future.* Such statements may not seem like vows, but they are infused with a significant emotional charge that locks them into the body. They then become integrated into the false identity that is built up by the mortal mind and they pass from conscious awareness. They may be forgotten but they persist. Such vows will indeed prevent us from engaging with life in any way that threatens to repeat an original traumatic experience, or limit us to repeating a particular joyful one in such a way that it becomes monotonous and prevents new discoveries.

The salient point to remember about all vows is that they are powerful statements of intent, so they are imbued with our energy until we reclaim it. Sometimes they take a lot of detective work to uncover, but it is important to do this work. The other main thing to remember with them is that they serve to reinforce imprints, and vice versa. So once a particular imprint has been seen and the energies reclaimed and transmuted, it is necessary to dissolve any associated vow.

In my experience whenever we come up against a solid obstruction in our personal development process we have hit a vow. Whenever we feel as if we just cannot get through our resistance, that whatever is holding us back is insurmountable we have hit a vow. Whenever there is an outright internal *no* in relation to a situation that we want to explore there is always a vow underneath the difficulty. This makes vow-breaking, or some process that implicitly neutralizes redundant vows and their effects, vital to progressing through our personal issues.

As with imprinting, the catalogue that follows is only intended to expand the concept of what vows are and how they might originate. This in its turn is meant to assist in developing an awareness of vows and to help put them in perspective. It is not a definitive list or a formal classification, neither is it in any way a condemnation of any vow or the intent behind it.

IMPLICIT VOWS

Implicit vows are mental body interpretations of our primal programming. This programming is deep in the cellular memory and originates in the genetic coding that we inherit from our non-human ancestry – our animal instincts. These instincts are, of course, invaluable but they also constitute limitations to our expression when they are translated out of their context. They become vows. And because they are so deeply rooted in a primitive past, when they surface they are often completely irrational in relation to the circumstances that trigger them. Nevertheless they can produce very intense emotional reactions as they have an imperative quality that is underwritten by survival fears. These vows are of the kind listed here ...

- To procreate for the survival of the species, even though I am violated or sacrificed in the process
- To defend my territory against all strangers and intruders
- To protect those who are dependent upon me
- To continue to feed and fatten-up beyond my needs for fear of starvation ... (survival)
- To compete for the purpose of mating and breeding
- To conceal myself in order to avoid discovery (by a predator) ...

None of these vows is wrong in itself, or in the context of species perpetuation. However they can inform many behavior patterns that sabotage our consciousness and inhibit our growth. For example a vow to defend a territory can feed a predisposition to create of enemies where there are none; a vow to conceal myself can turn into reclusiveness and isolation which will sustain any abandonment issue; a vow to procreate can turn into a predatory preoccupation with sex.

VIRTUAL VOWS

These are vows that generally come from feeling a need to protect our sensitivity. They are made unconsciously very early on in life as a response to the overwhelming onslaught of the physical world. As such they may have been made before there was a linguistic ability to articulate what it was we were choosing more of, or choosing to stop, so they are more like self-imposed energy structures that we determine to exist within rather than vows. Nevertheless they operate as vows and respond to the vow-breaking process.

As a means of self-protection these structures serve us well, particularly at a time when we are unable to control our environment. Typically these structures can be articulated in the form of vows as follows:

- To shut myself down ... or numb myself out ... in order to prevent myself feeling the violence, chaos and lack of love around me
- Never to allow my true self to be revealed in the environment of violence and lovelessness that I perceive around me
- To allow myself to express only in ways that validate my existence and produce a feeling of comfort and safety (this is a *virtual* vow to support and conform to the consensus reality)
- To take the pain of my environment as my responsibility and do everything I can to compensate for it

VOWS OF DISEMPOWERMENT

These are essentially vows of self-suppression, which is often confused with self-control. Self-control, however, is an ability that has a quality of consciousness associated with it. Self-suppression is the psychological equivalent of self-harm.

All vows are ultimately disempowering, but those that follow here are rooted in the fear of our own power and a rejection of our creative responsibility. This is the fear that some great disaster or tragedy will ensue from standing in our own power and creating our reality consciously. This fear could be very real, coming from a time when we did in fact create something that looked like devastation. To ensure that this can never happen again we assign our authority to an external source and suffer this to override our own inner wisdom and values. Vows that are formalized within a social order with phrases like *on my honor, by almighty God* and *by all that is sacred*, also fall into this category.

These vows come from severe self-criticism, and from interpreting the consequences of our own actions without compassion. They may prevent us from messing up again, but they also prevent us from healing any trauma we might still carry from such events because they prevent us venturing into similar territory ever again. The substance of these kinds of vows is typically as listed below:...

- Never to share my truth – thoughts, wisdom or understanding
- Never to express as an autonomous instrument of spirit or higher intelligence
- Never to trust myself (to place my trust in a 'wiser' external authority – for the good of all)
- To trust myself only when I am validated externally – by the state or by my peers
- To ignore my intuition and my inner wisdom
- To see the enemies/friends of my peers (or the state) as my enemies/friends
- To exact revenge as a form of justice (to assuage my own pain and trauma by re-inflicting it on others)
- Never to use my power again to consciously create any reality
- Never to allow myself to occupy or inhabit a position where it is possible for me to use my power to consciously create a reality
- Never to allow myself to occupy or inhabit a position where I experience my disempowerment as a physical reality (ensure I have no power and therefore avoid the anguish of disempowerment)
- Never to influence others through sharing my wisdom and teaching
- Never to allow myself to occupy or inhabit a position where it is possible for my wisdom and teaching to be shared and disseminated

Some of the vow structures above have a double-bind quality, which can actually apply to almost any vow. Double bind vows are a particular energy formation designed to lock in the basic vow against the possibility arising that it can become conscious and available to be rescinded. Linguistically these vows take the form ... *never to allow myself to occupy a position where it is possible for me to* ... or ... *to express in contradiction of the vow of.* These structures can really be regarded as a safeguard against the achievement of an appropriate level of consciousness before the vow can be released. Determining where a double-bind condition persists is largely a matter of feeling and intuition.

ETERNAL VOWS

One of the characteristics of eternal vows is that they have a tendency to bleed through from lifetime to lifetime. This is particularly true when an event results in our death, or the death of someone else, and we make a *never/always* decision in that moment. These vows are locked in place with a death-imprint, the energetic residue of the shock of the incident. Other kinds of vow that bleed through are the kind that we make to God – which are essentially vows to our own soul, and solemn blood vows of the kind associated with cloistered and esoteric orders and fraternities. These vows nearly always have a residual effect in the current incarnation until they are formally rescinded.

Mostly the vows relating to monastic brotherhoods or sisterhoods, religious orders, fraternities, and secret societies are those of renunciation: vows that imply a high degree of self-sacrifice ...

• Humility
• Obedience
• Silence
• Poverty
• Celibacy
• Chastity
• Self-sacrifice
• Self-denial
• Solitude

- Seclusion
- To take responsibility for the circumstances of others – feelings, pain or suffering

Other vows in this category can be considered largely as vows of allegiance in respect of or to uphold a particular ... planetary, international, national, ethnic, racial, religious, political, ideological, esoteric ... systematization of belief or code of ethics. It is not difficult to see vows of this kind at work in the everyday world we live in, nor how they can blight our self-expression unconsciously.

Just as with the other lists in this chapter, it is to be recognized that this list of vows is not exhaustive, neither is it universal. That is to say it does not apply in its entirety to any one individual, although almost everyone will resonate very strongly with some of the inclusions. Wherever you feel a sense of tightening inside it is likely that the item is relevant to your process – the *principle of in-formation and in-tuition* is in operation, trust it and give intent to explore what it has to say to you. When you are ready you can create a sacred space for yourself and use the procedures below to address whatever you have found.

PRACTICAL

Before embarking on any of this work you must first center yourself as described previously in chapter four. Then create a sacred space for yourself using the format given in chapter seven. Remember all procedures are to be spoken aloud.

As always with any feeling and emotional content that surfaces, simply let it be there. Go into the witness state in the subtle space *behind* the feeling or emotion. Stay as fully present as you can and watch the feeling evaporate: practice *the principle of presence*.

Also note that all of the processes and formats given in this book are founded on the *principle of universal wisdom*. So anything that pops into your mind when you speak these aloud is significant: it may be a direct reference to some incident; it may be an associated sense or feeling; it may be a metaphor for something that needs to be addressed. Pay attention to whatever comes, and if you need more clarity ask (*Spirit*) for it.

BASIC FORMAT FOR CUTTING EMOTIONAL TIES

> ➤ Spirit, please work with me at every level Physical, Mental, Emotional and Spiritual, and work holographically throughout all lifetimes, all realities, all dimensions and forms of existence ...
>
> Please completely remove the energy of ... < **NAME of the other person** > ... especially his/her ... **fear, anger, control, jealousy, judgment, criticism, pain, neediness, grief, expectation, shame, guilt, projection** ... etc ... from every aspect of my being ...
>
> And work with ... < **NAME of the other person** > ... in the most appropriate way for him/her ... And completely remove my energy ... especially the energy of my **fear, anger, control** ... etc ... from every aspect of his/her being ...
>
> Replace all of this ... in both of us ... with Divine Love, Truth and Wisdom ...

For particularly intense and abusive relationship situations it's a good idea to insert an intent for karmic release as follows:

> ➤ I call upon Archangel Michael and the Law of Grace to balance all karma between us with Compassion and Wisdom ...

The last part of the process is to express your gratitude for the learning experience and speak to the essence of the other as if they are present affirming the reclamation of your energy :

> ➤ Dear ... < **NAME** > ... **thank-you** for being my friend ... lover ... husband ... brother ... mother ... etc ... whatever I took on from you I surrender to return to its source right now ... I give

you permission to make ay mistakes you need to make ...
[to be who you are as truly as possible] ... as you follow your
soul's path wherever it leads ...

And I claim my energy for myself to follow wherever my
soul leads ... [whether you like it or not] ...

For very persistent attachments it is sometimes necessary to add
a further two stages. The first is to break any promise or vow you
might have made 'always to be *there*' for someone. The second is to
dispatch any astral entities that may have been assigned to sustain
the attachment. The vow break goes like this:

> ➤ I ... < **insert full birth name** > ... rescind, revoke, abandon
> and forswear any vow, contract, covenant, oath, promise,
> decision or agreement I have made ... anyone in my spiritual
> or genetic lineage has made ... consciously or unconsciously
> ... to take responsibility for the feelings and welfare of any
> other being, particularly < **NAME** > ...
>
> ... to **'always be there'** for < **NAME** > or any other being ...
> ... to sacrifice my needs in the interest of those of another
> ...
>
> I declare these vows, contracts, covenants, oaths,
> promises, decisions and agreements totally null and void ... in
> this incarnation and all incarnations across space and time,
> across all universes, all realities, all dimensions and the Great
> Void without exception. And so it is.

Unwanted astral entities are dispatched with gratitude for the work
they have done in holding whatever behavior pattern or program to
you. They can be regarded as thought-forms that have evolved their
own self-sustaining capability supported by your energy. As such
they are conscious intelligences in your service supporting the way
you chose to survive, and evolving from your need. They are also,
therefore, implicated in assisting you to honor your own mastery.
They are NOT little 'nasties' sent to punish you, or evil parasitic
creatures preying on you, but they are sustained by your energy. The

command process is as follows:

> ➤ I ... withdraw any permission I have given ... anyone in
> my spiritual or genetic lineage has given ... consciously or
> unconsciously ... for any being entity, parasite, consciousness
> or intelligence connected with ... < **NAME** >...or for ...
> < **NAME** > ... him/herself ... to attach to me or inhabit my
> body in any way ... And I direct all these to leave now and
> return to their source in the optimum way for us all ... and
> I call upon Archangel Michael and the Law of Grace for
> assistance with this.

There can be a lot of fear surface with this stage as the entity
realizes the source of its support is withdrawn. It feels its survival
threatened. You will feel this fear as if it is yours. Be present with it
and let it move through.

There are two important conditions to be observed when
cutting ties like this. The first is that cutting ties between parents
and children has to be relative to the age of the child. Children are
seldom ready for this until at least they are past puberty.

The second is that it is virtually imperative to cut ties in all sexual
relationships. Orgasm is a deeply imprinting energy, as the charge
present in any sexual connection derives from the deepest expression
of who we are whether we are aware of it or not. As always intuition
is the guiding light, and in order to take personal prejudices out of
the equation a form of words can be introduced to hold the intent
up to *Spiritual Intelligence* for moderation:

> ➤ ... in the optimum way for everyone involved ... in the
> most appropriate way to support our evolution ... if this is
> appropriate at this time.

One other point to note is that couples who divorce often still find
themselves caught up in the emotional wrangles of blame and
revenge years after they've moved on to other relationships. Cutting
emotional ties will always be effective in this situation, but it should

also be remembered that the marriage ceremony involves making vows to each other. These need to be revoked.

BASIC FORMAT FOR RELEASING IMPRINTS

〰 Spirit, please work with me at every level: Physical, Mental, Emotional and Spiritual, ... work holographically throughout all lifetimes, all realities, all dimensions and forms of existence ... and work with my Cellular Memory ... my Ancestral Memory ... my Soul Memory (Akashic Record) ...

Work also with my mind and mental body, and my emotional body...

EITHER

Please completely neutralize any imprint that I carry that causes me to think, feel, believe or behave as if ... [Here insert the condition that has been identified ... e.g. 'my wisdom/ creativity is of zero value.]

OR

Please cancel and dissolve any imprint that I carry that causes me to ...

... identify myself as ...

... identify myself with any particular practice... expression ... possession ... group ...

... incorporate the characteristics of ... into my identity ...

Melt away all the tension, trauma, fear, pain, despair ... any of this has ever created in me ... and transmute all of these energies into Divine Love, Divine Light, Divine Truth and Divine Wisdom ... [... other qualities like compassion, expression, passion and freedom can be included here ...]

This procedure can be augmented with vow breaks and entity removals as above, where it FEELS relevant, as some of these conditions are locked deeply into our identity structures. The need for such additions becomes apparent with practice.

BASIC FORMAT FOR BREAKING
REDUNDANT VOWS

The vow-breaking format given in the procedure for cutting emotional ties is specific for that application. A more general formulation is as follows:

> ➤ I ... < **insert full birth name** > ... rescind, revoke, renounce, abandon and forswear any vow ... [contract, covenant, oath, agreement, promise or decision] ... I have made ... anyone in my spiritual or genetic lineage has made ... consciously or unconsciously ...
>
> ... < here insert the nature of the vow or decision to be revised > ...
>
> *[It's possible to string a list of associated vows together in this structure]*
>
> ... I declare these vows ... [contracts, covenants, oaths, agreements, promises and decisions] ... totally null and void ... without exception ...in this incarnation and all incarnations across space and time, across all universes, all realities, all dimensions and the Great Void. And so it is.

10.

Presence

As soon as you trust yourself,
you will know how to live.

JOHANN WOLFGANG VON GOETHE
(1749 – 1832)

SPIRITUALLY INTELLIGENT PERSPECTIVES

It took me a long time to understand that spiritually intelligent perspectives have very little in common with the prevalent consensus way of looking at things. Spiritually intelligent perspectives look inward and seek to bring my awareness into my own creative power. They support my own life force and its unique expression. And they also support everyone else in the expression of their unique mastery.

When I am fully present to what is, without desiring to change it in any way, without judging it in any way, the polarities of right and wrong become irrelevant. But – and this is really important – I have to be present to what is in relation to myself alone, and nobody else.

Whatever the situation nobody else is relevant to my experience; it is my experience not theirs. They will be having their own experience, which is relevant to them alone, even though there may be an interchange between us. I first became aware of this many years ago...

> When my son was 12 years old he developed type one diabetes. I was shocked and devastated. I wept and wept. I saw the potential threat to his young life, and I would readily have taken the burden myself if I could. I had a major attack of self-pity: how could this be happening to me? How could life be so cruel? Then I realized it wasn't happening to me, it was happening to him. Moreover the world would keep turning no matter what I felt or believed about the situation.
>
> Suddenly I understood that nothing had happened to me and that I could do nothing about what had happened to my son. This produced a strange sense of gratitude in me. Initially there was also a sense of shame that I could feel this as a consequence of such a distressing situation. Then I saw that my gratitude had nothing to with being glad that someone else had suffered an injury whilst I had escaped; it was gratitude for my own health, strength and vitality. It was ok for me to have these feelings; it did not make me a monster.
>
> It was my son's burden to live with this condition. He had to figure out how he would manage it for himself. He had to find what worked and what didn't. He had to learn to manage his health. It was a serious challenge for him, but it was his challenge and it was for him to overcome, and there was nothing I could do that would change that.
>
> All of this was a startling revelation to me. What I realized was that the best thing I could do was be the best me I could be, maintain integrity with myself – not something I was used to in those days. But I did my best, and gradually regenerated myself.
>
> In this way I was able to support my son in finding his own

way through his difficulties, as he grappled with the onset of adolescence and grew to manhood. As you might imagine this story has many turns and twists which all contained significant learning for everyone concerned. However the underlying truth that I learned for myself was that by empowering myself I empowered him.

> *When you empower yourself you empower*
> *everyone around you.*

When I first learned this I had no concept of *Spiritual Intelligence*, let alone a spiritually intelligent perspective. Now I regularly tend to ask myself the question: Is there a soul perspective that makes sense of my situation? I find myself considering the possibility that, in spite of the apparent chaos, conflict and distress I see in the world, my soul actually sets up potentials for me choose to act out.

The more I look at myself and the world I live in the more convinced I am that this is indeed what my soul does. It does this so that I can come to my own appreciation of the mystery that lives in me, so that I can discover my own sense of myself. How I act out the various potentials physically, mentally and emotionally is my choice, and this is what determines the form – but not the content – of the next set of potentials coming my way.

My soul, the *essence of my presence*, is actually waiting for me to ask the questions and *feel* the answers that come from within me. The *essence of my presence* is waiting for me to see that the only explanation that makes sense of the chaos is that it is there for me to use as a signpost on the way to my own truth.

None of this has anything to do with some kind of pre-ordained destiny, which makes a nonsense of the *principle of alignment* and free will. My *essence* is only interested in my journey to a place of alignment, because that's where the learning lies. My essence continues to seek to provoke my curiosity about the mystery of my self-presence allowing me to draw to myself situations that will facilitate this provocation, and give me more opportunities to empower myself.

Once I commit to embodying as much of my *essence* as possible, the frequency and intensity of the opportunities that will pull me deeper into myself increase. These will also show me the validity of the process through the expansion and joy that I experience as I come more into alignment with my *essence*.

I am still quite free to decide that there is no sense to anything, and if this is my decision chaos, frustration and dysfunction will continue, proving the veracity of my judgment. However, if I decide that everything serves a purpose, which my soul is aware of yet somehow I may have missed, things begin to make sense. This also proves the veracity of my judgment, which leaves me with a conundrum, because whatever I decide is true will be verified by my experience. But what this situation really tells me is that I am in charge of me and how I experience myself, which means I am in charge of my life whether I like it or not.

The recipe for developing a spiritually intelligent perspective can be summarized in the following affirmations:

- Everything that happens externally in my life is a reflection of my inner state.
- Whenever I take something personally my reaction is an indication that the current expression of who I think I am is out of integrity with the core essence that I am.
- Everything I perceive in my world reality has an archetypal significance (or meta-significance), which is only revealed when I am in a place of emotional detachment.
- At a rarified level we are all part of the same consciousness, which is another way of saying there is only one being in the universe. This means that every interaction I have with another is an interaction with a representative of a part of myself, and the awareness or otherwise of anyone else involved is irrelevant to my process.
- There is only Love and Light in all of existence, where these are absent we say there is fear and darkness.

If you're looking for an easy way out of life's dilemmas and crises, spiritually intelligent perspectives have nothing to offer. Reframing our experiences, and our interpretation of our experiences, to develop a spiritually intelligent perspective is a compelling endeavor that will reveal many places of resistance and denial, if we choose to look. It offers a way through the mystery of the shadow transforming fear into wisdom. This initially brings greater acceptance, understanding and compassion. In the wake of this comes joy and delight as the great cosmic joke of taking ourselves too seriously is penetrated.

THE LIGHT, THE DARK AND THE SHADOW

The light and the dark are terms often used to denote the basic polarity of good and evil. The shadow is a term that originates in Jungian psychology and which refers to an amorphous unconscious repository of what we fear and dislike in ourselves. The shadow is the indeterminate space between light and dark where one shades into the other, the deeper the shadow the darker the nature of what lives there. However, if we consider the dark to be the absence of light we can begin to unpick this metaphor a little. The dark is not a facility we can bring to bear on the light to make it darker, but the light can shine into the dark, and where it does the darkness is eliminated.

Wherever there is a shadow it is cast by something standing in the way of the light. The brighter the sun shines, the harder the shadows. And when the light is really bright it can be difficult, if not impossible, to see anything beyond the intensity of the glare. When we want to see clearly in bright sunshine we seek the shade to look out from, and if we can't find any we create some with a hand to the eyes. So our experience of the phenomena of light and dark is that we can see things more clearly by standing in the shadow.

This is the allegory that we need to transfer to the inner process. The more the light of the soul shines through, the clearer will be the issues that inhabit the shadow, but we have to stand in the shade in order to see these clearly. We have to stop looking the other way.

If you've decided at some point that anger is bad, that it's responsible for pain in some way, then the chances are that you will suppress your anger. It could be a betrayal of your self-identity to express it. If you've decided that expressing what you want for yourself causes distress in those around you, you may have great difficulty in claiming anything for your personal needs. If you've decided that men are abusive, the chances are that you will reject any part of yourself you see as masculine; likewise if you've concluded that women can not be trusted in some way you will reject parts of yourself you see as feminine. All of this self-rejection lives on in the shadow.

The trouble is when we look inside most of us see things we not only wish weren't there, but often things we are thoroughly ashamed of. Some of these things will be thoughts and fantasies, and some will be memories of real events and situations. Because of the intense shame we feel about these things our automatic impulse is to bury them so deep within that they can never be seen in the light of day again. Then just for good measure we teach ourselves to forget about the burial, which successfully persuades us that what lies buried never was there in the first place. This enables us to continue living with ourselves, but somewhere within we know.

Everything that lives in the shadow is everything that we reject about ourselves, everything we refuse to love. It is everything about us that fails to comply with the ideal social specification of our self-identity; we are terrified it will be discovered and cause our downfall. We pretend it doesn't exist, but we know it's there, full of resentment for its denial, that's why there's such a widespread fear of the dark. To be truly conscious we must embrace the potential of the shadow individually and collectively. For as long as we continue in our efforts to deny it, it will keep manifesting destructively in various aspects of our lives.

The *principle of projection* tells us that when we kill our enemies we are really only killing representatives of the shadow parts of ourselves, parts we don't want to see. The representative may be gone but the shadow parts of ourselves are still there. This is why wars never settle anything. It is also why civil wars break out soon after a tyrannical or occupying regime is removed. With the old enemy gone society turns on itself and creates a new enemy. The existence of a common enemy is therefore often a stabilizing factor of the social order. For this reason alone commitment to your own personal empowerment is a service to all of humanity.

A spiritually intelligent perspective understands that the shadow is the facilitator of our growth. Its very existence is a sign that there is a purpose to our existence, that we have a job to do. When issues begin to surface out of the shadow it's not a sign that something is wrong, but quite the reverse. It may present us with a problem, but it's a sign that we are holding more of our light. The light is simply showing us where it is still blocked. We are being guided to the next step in the process of self-empowerment. Convention says we must find an answer so the problem goes away, wisdom says the problem is my friend trying to tell me something I'm reluctant to hear.

In itself, just opening up to the possibility that this might be an accurate assessment of the dynamic of the shadow is a huge shift out of the consensus rut. Giving intent to clear our shadow is the next step. Continuing this journey is to follow our own light, which will ultimately shine unimpeded.

Whenever the possibility arises that something we've consigned to the shadow in this way might be revealed to us – or worse, to others – we are likely to experience the emotional responses of fear and anger. Because we are normally in a condition of blissful ignorance of what's been hidden in the shadow, owing to the supreme efficiency of our denial process, these emotional responses can be intensely reactive. This is the surest sign that we've stumbled on an aspect of ourselves that requires understanding and compassion – something that really is *me* but which has been determined as incongruent with the self-identity I've constructed to present to myself and the world I live in.

The key to shifting all of the issues lurking in the shadow is the *principle of presence*. By staying present with anything that arises, remaining aware of our breathing and letting any feelings express we eventually feel the sadness locked into the part of ourselves we consigned to the shadow. We feel its mistrust, its fear and its abject loneliness. Simply allowing this to be present within is a process of acceptance, recognizing that it is all ok brings us a step closer to a realization of self-mastery. This is not necessarily easy, as has been indicated before, it takes courage and persistence. Gradually the shadow comes to be seen as the friend it truly is, and the issues it shows us are the keys to self-empowerment. This is its gift.

THE PARADIGM SHIFT

Anyone who has been paying attention to the underlying trends in western society over the last decade (or even two decades) cannot fail to notice that things are changing fast. There is an unprecedented wave of conscious awareness sweeping the world, and this is accompanied by an unprecedented wave of disaffection and violence. If we adopt a spiritually intelligent perspective we can see the phenomena we are witnessing as a demonstration of the interplay between light and dark, and as the outworking of the collective shadow showing us the level of collective denial. The gathering intensity indicates that what we are living through is a great awakening in consciousness. If this finds coherence it cannot but generate a new paradigm. However that paradigm can only be guessed at until it manifests itself.

A spiritually intelligent perspective recognizes the wave of awareness as a function of the Light, which throws the shadow into deeper contrast; the more light there is, the more intense is the shadow. What this signifies is that there is simply more of the *essence of our presence* available to all of us, and it is pushing us all to commit to it and allow it to express. This is the nature of the Light. What it is insistently showing us is the level of disparity, contradiction, disconnection, denial and general unconsciousness that permeates the way we live in the world. Our priorities are out of alignment – individually and collectively, nationally and internationally.

We are also being shown that doing things the way we are used to, out of our own strength, offers no lasting solutions to our predicament. Attempting social control by the imposition of force and might simply aggravates an already dysfunctional situation. It is the way we as humanity have conducted our affairs for a long time. It has never been the best way to support our evolution, but we have never been shown so clearly that it is not working. This is the old paradigm; it has brought us to where we are now and we are being asked to recognize its redundancy. We are being asked to shift the foundation of the reality we live in.

One of the problems with shifting is that we can't see where to shift to. So far all the possibilities do not look real, and we've lived with our present convention of reality for a long time. However, as the nature of reality still confounds our greatest minds we can safely say that no-one really knows what it is and no-one understands it, which means that what we presently call reality has no primacy. Nevertheless in order to shift we've literally got to take a step in the dark. This is what keeps us in the rut of doing things from what we think we know. And we are so disconnected from our true knowing that there are relatively few to lead the way.

Humanity has been, and largely still is disconnected from many subtle aspects of itself, intelligent non-physical aspects, which have to be acknowledged as inherently spiritual. For centuries this has been the province of religion, esoteric orders, and more recently the New Age movement. Quantum physics now shows us a potentially more pragmatic insight into this area. But this is still only a potential as the rarefied intellectual nature of quantum physics itself tends to ensure that it remains an area of mystery to the public at large. Quantum physics is still the province of experts and academics, which means it is effectively maintained as an instrument of mass disempowerment, and the truth it heralds is still denied.

Another problem for many seekers is the surfeit of information in support of the idea that we are at the dawn of a new age. This is something that has been prophesied for thousands of years, and is supported by research into many ancient aboriginal and spiritual traditions, including that of the Maya, the Hopi, and the Book of Revelation amongst many others. What most popular interpretations tell us is that we must change our ways or else. That is to say we are pressured to change the way we live in the world through the threat of catastrophe, retribution and fear. This apocalyptic visionary approach is still rooted in the old paradigm, the paradigm the visionaries themselves tell us we are moving out of. Because of this it is never going to be an effective strategy if we are truly moving into a new paradigm.

Yet, when the affairs of the world are interpreted from a spiritually intelligent perspective, the indications are that a new paradigm is evolving. Nobody really knows what the new paradigm is because it's up to us to create it. For it to be effective in any way it has to be based on alignment, but it cannot be imposed it has to emerge organically. I would suggest the list below offers some indication of the direction we are moving in.

Old Paradigm	New Paradigm
Separation	Connection
Force	Power
Control	Empowerment
Imposition	Immanence
Doubt	Trust (no how)
Knowledge (know-how)	Wisdom
Idealism	Authenticity
Violation	Respect
Blame	Self-responsibility
Polarization	Inclusion

SELF-EMPOWERMENT

Self-empowerment is standing in your own power. It is not the same thing as physical strength, nor is it power that can be exercised over anyone else. It is the ability to be centered within, to remain unaffected by whatever is happening around you and yet to feel your own responses and to act in away that maintains your integrity. It is the ability to stay out of your head and operate from a place of calm when things look like they're going wrong – curiously this is seen as keeping your head in some elements of society. It is the confidence to stand for yourself and allow others to stand for themselves.

Empowerment is about allowing the power of the universe to flow through you and trusting yourself to allow this, even if it doesn't look the way you expect. It's about surrendering the need to make something happen out of your own strength, even if this seems to be a sign of having no will-power. Too often the individual will is driven by the agenda of the mortal mind, which is seldom aligned with *Spiritual Intelligence.* What this amounts to is that will-power turns out to be a synonym for force – forcing ourselves, and others, to comply with what looks like it's good for us. To be empowered is to engage with what is good for us no matter what it looks like

Richard is a sensitive, caring and conscious man. He is totally committed to his own personal empowerment process, to cleaning up any abusive old-male behavior patterns and to living in harmony with the earth. As part of his own regime he paid great attention to his diet. He would eat only organic whole and live foods, avoided meat, chemicals of all description and alcohol, and maintained an advised intake of vitamin supplements. The trouble was Richard was getting sick.

Richard is a young man in his prime, yet his health and vitality had been dramtically fading over quite a short period. He went to see dieticians, specialists, complementary therapists and healers and did everything they told him. He would often feel a small improvement but soon his condition would continue on its downward spiral. As time went on it became apparent to him that he was literally dying. It seemed he had some pernicious debilitating condition that no-one could diagnose, and it seemed obvious there was no cure. He surrendered himself to his process not knowing where it was leading, and being fully aware that he may soon be leaving his earthly body.

But Richard was getting help from within. He kept having visions of a huge unhealthy pizza full of chemicals and processed bits of the corpses of animals, and of a big jug of beer. Both of these items were icons to Richard of just the kind of concept of manhood that he was moving out of, so he treated the visions as telling him what to stay away from. They were poisons that he knew his body was better off without. He figured they were simply items that his mind was showing him as a test, and he had to prove his integrity by resisting. The visions persisted and his condition worsened.

Eventually he thought to himself: *Well if I'm dying anyway a beer and a pizza will hardly make things worse.* So he gave in to what he thought was his mortal mind. One night when he thought the end must be close, he ordered the largest, ugliest, pizza he could and a cold beer. He consumed these somewhat nervously, but really enjoyed them. The next morning he woke up feeling better than he had for months. He was amazed, yet he understood the spiritually intelligent perspective he had been led to.

Richard had been forcing himself to do what he thought was right, what he had been advised by conscious people he respected and what fitted the concept he had of himself as a new man. But he had ignored his intuition. He had been giving his power away to people he thought had greater knowledge than he did, and to ideas that stemmed from his own rejection of what he saw as abusive male energy.

On the surface Richard's intuition was telling him he had to change to a diet of pizza and beer to be in good health. Underneath this the message was quite different, he was being told to empower himself and live, or die, with the consequences. He was being told to stop forcing himself to comply with ideals and concepts of perfection and to trust his own inner guidance. He is in fact now in the best of health and eating as consciously as ever.

There is a profound irony in this story; it is a reminder that the Light is light in more than one sense. The more guidance Richard was seeking outside himself, the more he was getting from within. *Spiritual Intelligence* was teasing him, daring him to break the rules he had bound himself with. What would have happened had he failed to hear his intuition finally? Who knows? But the message for us all is that our expectations, our ideals, our notions of propriety and even our concept of what is spiritual can all be blocks to our self-empowerment and the connection with *Spiritual Intelligence*.

Another point to be aware of that arises from this story is that force is an old paradigm way of getting things done. Moreover, force never really works because it inherently suppresses. This means it is an agency that serves the creation and maintenance of the shadow. Individually, repression and, collectively, suppression are the progenitors of oppression. They foster resentment and resistance. Whatever is implemented through force finds compliance through fear, fear of consequences and reprisal. This does not affirm life, but stifles it.

PRINCIPLES AND PRACTICE

If you've been following the exercises and processes in this book you'll have discovered lots about yourself that you weren't aware of. You've probably found a few issues to work on, and maybe even cleared a few. It's reasonable to expect that you are now ready to take another look at the thirteen principles of self-empowerment given in chapter one, and explore how you can engage with them pro-actively to support you in your own personal growth program.

The Principle of Interconnection

We are all subtly interconnected with the entirety of creation. Some of these connections are more obvious than others. Our local environment is the home of our strongest links and influences, which work in both directions – from them to us, and from us to them. But it is not just with other people that our interconnection exists, it is with everything else – the air, the earth, the water, our homes, possessions, the places we work and those we frequent for other purposes.

In Practice

⟿ Whenever you feel your mood change for no apparent reason, that is to say you've not just been pulled out of your center by some difficult incident or personal interaction, it's safe to assume that you're picking up something from your surroundings. It is a complete waste of energy to try to process your way through this because it is not yours to process. Pay attention to the atmosphere, the background energy, in your environment. Check it by changing your physical disposition: leave the room; leave the building; walk on a different street or cross the road. Watch how you feel before, after and as you make the change. If you feel better then you know for sure that what you were feeling was not yours.

Remember you can also be affected by world events, national celebrations and disasters. These are less easy to check in the way mentioned above. If you can, check the news, and ask yourself inside: *Is what I feel right now mine?* Do this particularly if what you feel is sadness, sorrow or depression. You will always get an answer, although you may have to practice a bit. Also if you ask *Spirit* for assistance with your discernment you will find that you keep finding yourself feeling what is around you at ever more sensitive levels.

The Principle of In-Formation and In-Tuition

The intelligence of the *Field* is constantly present within and around us. It is *in*-forming us all the time through the quanta that make up our atomic and molecular structure, our genetic coding and the subtle forces and thought-fields that act upon us. Virtually all of this goes unnoticed, and it's as well because the information overload would be too much for us to handle. But this is what creates the intuitions and insights that will be our guides into the unknown.

In Practice

➤ Intuitions can come in any form and generally correspond with our basic physical senses – visual, auditory, tactile, olfactory and gustatory. Sometimes there can be a physical manifestation like a brief visual disturbance, an itch, a cough, a twitch, a tingle, a pain. Insights are those epiphanous and inspired moments when things suddenly fall into place and make sense.

Any of these phenomena can be interrogated. Remember they are often archetypal and metaphorical representations. Something that you regard as a pain in the butt can produce just that. Your *Spiritual Intelligence* has no sense of shame because it knows everything is divine. A procedure for interrogation would be to say something like...

> *Spirit, please intensify this **pain**. Infuse it with*
> *love and show me what is underneath that's trying*
> *to express, and do this now.*

Keep asking for help in discerning the responses you get. And if you get nothing, examine the qualities of that nothing. Another important practice is to pay attention to the condition of your heart chakra. The heart never lies and its communication is most easily recognized as a feeling inside your chest.

Energetically the heart has two main conditions open or closed. When the heart opens it feels like an expansion in the middle of the chest cavity. This is the heart's signal that whatever is in prospect is life affirming and nourishing. When the heart closes it feels like a contraction inside. The body wants to slump, and emotionally it feels depressing. This is the heart's signal that whatever is in prospect is undermining, and limits life. There is also a middle condition. This feels like a kind of stuckness, where the heart is on the point of opening but refusing. This is the signal that something true is present that reflects upon falsely held beliefs, values and operating paradigms.

The more you pay attention to your intuition the more accurately you will learn to read it. This will reduce your stress levels, increase your confidence and boost self-esteem.

The Principle of Universal Wisdom

The knowing certainty that arises from within me, with no rational logic is a manifestation of *Universal Wisdom*. It has nothing to do with my own cleverness or intellect. It comes in the moment of its requirement and when I express it I feel strong and solid in my own center. Yet it leaves me wondering where it came from, and how I knew it.

In Practice

➤ *Universal Wisdom* often surfaces in moments of difficulty when truth is needed, and where personal intellectual ability has run out of steam. When the mortal-mind has exhausted itself that is the time when *Universal Wisdom* at last has the space to expand into. So it seems to come out of the blue.

When there is nothing coming to say or do this is the time to say and do nothing, even if a conclusion seems to be needed for a situation. This may be just the time when the mortal mind is in panic over what to say or do, and there may even be people around making demands: *Well, don't just stand there. Do something!* Or: *Well, say something then!*

Having the confidence to remain still and present in these situations, refusing to be precipitated into action or any form of expression so as to fit in with a general atmosphere of confusion, creates exactly the condition where *Universal Wisdom* can reveal itself. And where the confidence is lacking still, a little practice at faking it will soon develop the facility.

The Principle of Creation and Manifestation

We are constantly conditioning the *Field* with our unconscious thought forms, with what we want and mostly with what we don't want. And because it is the nature of the *Field* to respond to our creative power, what we manifest mirrors back to us the confusion within the creator – and the creator is us, me and you. There is an extremely high consensus resistance to this truth, because it means we are responsible for the world we find ourselves living in and we want to blame someone else. This is the almost universal convention of self-disempowerment.

In Practice

≈ We've been refusing to take responsibility for our creation for generations, as much out of ignorance as fear and denial. So now we find ourselves living in and with the product of our unconscious self-disempowerment.

The most important aspect to engaging with this principle is to decide what you want, and focus your attention on that alone. It is crucial that you eliminate all negative linguistic formulations from this focus. It must not be driven by anything you do not want, and it must not be conceived of as an antithesis, that is to say it must be for rather than against. Furthermore it must be articulated only in direct way.

The only other process necessary is to give intent to reach the place where you experience what you want and commit to taking any action necessary to get you there. Above all it is imperative that you do not try to adhere to your own plan of the journey, but simply take the steps one at a time as they are revealed to you. Your own plan may well be a useful starting point, but it will stifle your creative power if you try to stick to it rigidly.

The Principle of Self-Identity (Principle of Subjectivity)

The entire artifice of human culture is founded on this principle. So it is not something that allows an easy escape from its government. In fact it has to be allowed if you are to have any meaningful interaction with other human beings. But to be conscious of it is to be free of its tyranny.

In Practice

≈ Be assured in the knowledge that very few people have any concept of who they are. Whoever you think you are is only a costume, an outfit that allows you to walk around the planet in a way that others here can relate to.

Become conscious of how you refer to yourself, particularly

when you say *I am* in relation to your emotions or the role you fulfill in society. Start reframing your expression. Instead of saying *I am very angry/sad/happy* say *I feel very angry/sad/happy*; instead of saying *I'm a lawyer/manager/carpenter* say *I work as a lawyer/manager/carpenter*. When asked to say who you are say *My name is* rather than *I am*. Adopt the Hebrew mantra *Ehyeh Asher Ehyeh*. This is usually translated as *I am that I am*, but could also be *I will be that which I will be*. Say this aloud to yourself every day.

As you become more conscious of the way you identify yourself with your situation and surroundings you will also become more aware that your true identity has nothing to do with either. You will become more present with the *essence* of who you are at your core. You will be more empowered and more effective in everything you do.

The Principle of Projection

Projection is a displacement activity that sites the locus of our power outside ourselves. Understand that everyone projects. It is the way we interact with the world through our mental faculty. We see the world as we are, and the world reflects our image back to us. When we don't like what we see we disown it, this is the root of all our problems.

In Practice

➤ A working knowledge of the *principle of projection* is one of the best tools we have at our disposal for our self-empowerment. If I know that I project I can commit to examining everything reflected back to me to see where I have my energy invested in ways that undermine me. This applies as much to what I like as to what I abhor. Staying centered on what I like can be a serious distraction from what really needs my attention.

A question to ask internally about any situation is *How is this me?* Then pay attention to the practices outlined above under the *principle of in-formation and in-tuition*. A particularly useful question with difficult situations that we want to reject is *Is this in me?* Then place your attention on any indication given by the heart chakra. If it feels stuck or numb you know you've found something that needs further exploration.

Also because you know everyone else is projecting you can ignore any criticism directed at you in the moment. It is always about the critic and although there may be some truth for you to address, it will not be relevant to the moment. It will be coming from a defensive position in the critic. This is also true when you criticize, so be aware that your criticism is an indication of self-rejection. Give intent to clear any of the issues you spot as they arise and this will continue to move you forward in your evolution.

The Principle of Reaction

Emotional reaction is always a response to a condition that either supports (a pleasurable reaction) or undercuts (a fearful reaction) any self-identity structure that you have taken on as an absolute truth. Along with projection, your emotional reaction is one of the most powerful tools you have at your disposal for empowering yourself.

In Practice

➤ Essentially your emotional reactions are demonstrations of the processes by which you disempower yourself. So noting them for attention and working through them has to bring you into a place of empowerment.

Know that your emotional reaction is a powerful friend, even if it is very uncomfortable. Developing the witness state to watch yourself while you experience your reaction and staying present with the feelings that arise is the key to moving forward. Make sure that you keep your breath moving and see if you can find a space behind the feeling to rest in whilst still feeling what is moving, because it is moving.

What you feel in this process situation is what is leaving. That is to say you are letting go of unexpressed emotional energy that has been held in your body. Gradually the triggers that set off your reaction will be cleared and you will hold your center more readily in any situation.

The Principle of Self-Awareness

Self-awareness is the quality we possess that allows us to know we are alive in an objective sense, and to self-analyze. It is self-awareness that makes it possible for me to see that my body is a separate entity from the *I* that inhabits it.

In Practice

≈ Notice how you observe your physical body. It is yours, which means you possess it. This is not possession in the sense of ownership, but in the sense of occupying or inhabiting. Spend some time getting comfortable with this.

Your body is not you, but it represents you and signifies your presence to you. It has its own natural intelligence which is generally wiser than the intellect, and much more honest. Notice how you refer to yourself and your body. The mortal mind will project much of its shadow onto the physical body.

Notice the internal dialogues and debates you have within yourself. Who are these entities? How does it feel when they are talking to you? And if they do talk to you, who or what is the you they are talking to?

Your awareness of all of this is that you. It is the transcendental consciousness of who you are that will never be identified by the strategies and constructs of the mortal-mind. The more you are able to recognize this presence within you the more self-empowered you will be.

The Principle of Responsibility

This is the principle that we are all empowered by when we

acknowledge it, and disempowered by when we ignore it. It insists that we have the intrinsic ability to create the life we lead; we have the intrinsic ability to choose the way we interact with our circumstances and change them by changing within. It is not, however, about apportioning blame, but recognizing that there is no blame.

In Practice

> ≋ Understand that the only person you can ever change is yourself. Stop trying to change other people so that they fit into boxes that sit well in your comfort zone. Stop trying to control situations to prevent yourself feeling uncomfortable.
>
> Instead, look within. Give yourself permission to be discomforted, to be judgmental and resentful, and ask where those feelings are really coming from. What are the pet ideas that are being challenged? What are the dangers you don't want to face? Is there any way you can look at the world differently to bring yourself to a deeper understanding of a situation?
>
> Try saying to yourself *I know I've created this situation somehow so it must be showing me something I need to see.* Give intent to see your own part clearly in any situation and accept it. Desist from pointing out anyone else's.
>
> Make these your guidelines and you will see more and more just where your responsibility lies. Opening up to this will support your self-empowerment process totally.

The Principle of Separation

This principle can be considered as an inversion of the *principle of interconnection*. It derives from interpreting the discrete intelligence of my mortal-mind as an isolated entity. This is of course only effectively true for as long as my mortal mind holds on to its illusion. However, whilst the mortal mind is in total control, or believes it is, the *principle of separation* is the source of much conflict.

In Practice

➮ Understand that all feelings of separation, isolation, loneliness and abandonment come from an interpretation of circumstances based on incomplete information. Even if you have difficulty believing this, open to the possibility that it is true. The exclusion of the subtle fields of *in*-formation is a consequence of the dominance of physical phenomena and their overwhelming of any subtle perceptions. This is the largest contributory factor to the conceptualization of yourself in separation.

Notice how you feel in relation to world events, and stop making excuses for what you feel. Tune in to someone you know well and see if you can feel what their emotional or mental state is.

Give yourself an opportunity to feel your connectedness with all life by truly desiring it and asking *Spirit* for a demonstration. Say aloud:

> *Spirit, please work with me at every appropriate*
> *subtle level. Connect with me now so that I can*
> *feel my essence within me as part of the universal*
> *whole.*

Then watch what happens. Do this until you really feel it and stop pretending to yourself that you feel nothing.

The Principle of Approval

This principle shows us the agency by which we give our power away to external authorities: parents, teachers, priests, institutions, governments and our friends. In some ways it's our friends and the relationships we have with them that are the most insidious, as it's through their approval that we validate our existence. Whatever part of ourselves we give away through our lack of authenticity in any social context we find justification for through our friends and the social acceptance they afford us.

In Practice

➤ Realize that you have been seeking approval for most of your life, and because of this you have compromised your integrity time and time again. Understand that you were doing your best all the time and that if there had seemed to be a viable alternative you would have taken it.

Notice any self-judgment that arises from this, and disregard it. This is simply your mortal mind reacting to the potential that it's been getting things wrong, and if it's been getting things wrong it's not going to get the approval it needs to validate itself.

Give intent to stop seeking approval, and to stop apologizing for being the way you are. Then use the formats given in the earlier chapters to ask *Spirit* for help in dismantling the programming and the behavior patterns that cause you to validate yourself through approval – either that of yourself or another.

Pay attention to anywhere that you seek to relate to another person through a dynamic of approval and stop it. Trust that the relationship will support you in this – if you are freed from needing approval so will they be.

The Principle of Alignment

Being in alignment means to be connected with my essence and centered in whatever it is that brings me to life. This is the place of passion and enthusiasm. When we live in alignment we thrive and prosper. The universe is dedicated to aliveness and is constantly regenerating itself. Anything that doesn't thrive fades away and dies by the very nature of things, its energy to be recycled in support of what is moving and growing. Being in alignment takes nothing from anyone else. It is not about contriving my success at the expense of another. Being in alignment, I can feel the energy of the universe supporting the life that finds its full expression in me.

In Practice

↝ The practice for getting into alignment can be summed up as: find out what makes you feel alive and do more of it; and find out what depresses you and dump it. Use your heart chakra to discern anything that you have no enthusiasm for. Whatever it is that closes you down with gloom and despondency, abandon it; it is a drain on your life force.

Give yourself permission to find out what you are passionate about, and own it. If this is still a bit of a mystery to you, follow anything that gives you a feeling of expansion in your heart. Passion is a greatly misunderstood energy, it is the purest expression of who you are that you can connect with in a physical body, but it has been confused with irrational and violent acts. It is only when it is suppressed that its expression is distorted. Your heart will not lead you astray, although it may run you into a little trouble with your mortal mind. If you are really shut down in this area ask for help. Say aloud:

> *Spirit, please work with me at every level, physical,*
> *mental, emotional and spiritual. Go deep into my*
> *cellular memory and dismantle any structure that*
> *disconnects me from my passion. Work with my*
> *mind, my mental body and my emotional body*
> *and dissolve any mind-set or thought-form that*
> *causes me to believe my passion is dangerous and*
> *transmute all of the energies committed to these*
> *processes into Divine Love, Divine Truth and*
> *Divine Wisdom.*

Trust the process and expect things to move. Connecting with your passion is essential to empowering yourself.

Be ruthless with yourself in where you allow your energy to focus, but stay out of judgment. Just because your energy does not find its match in a particular situation or with a particular group that does not mean that the people in that situation are better or worse than you. It simply means there's not a match. Situations and relationships change and evolve.

The Principle of Presence

To be fully present is to be totally in your body, totally alive, totally in tune with your surroundings and totally in the moment, what Eckhart Tolle calls the *Now*[8]. This is where you are empowered. It is the only point where you can be effective, where you can act. You cannot act in the future or the past. Whatever you do it will be *now* when you do it. Dwelling on the future and the past is a distraction that drains your energy from where it is most effective.

When you are fully present, your presence affects everything and everyone around you. It is an energy that demands that it is matched. Through simple resonance, it will pull other people into their own center and facilitate their experience of their own presence – it will bring them more present with themselves. Anything that is not a match will simply fall away.

In Practice

➚ Being present is simple, but it's far from easy. There are thousands of distractions every second. Every time you follow one of these you have lost the quality of presence. Know this and do not despair.

Notice where you are in your mind at all times, and whatever you are doing just do it. When you are driving, drive; when you are eating, eat; when you are walking, walk. If you are ironing a shirt, don't figure out the shopping list at the same time, just iron the shirt. In this way everything you do becomes a meditation.

Above all refrain from reprimanding yourself. When you do this you are present with your mortal mind, not your essence. This means you are present with your own inner critic and this will only get you down.

Spend time with people committed to their own self-empowerment. You will not only create an energy field that supports and sustains each other, you will provide a facility that others can tune into. Thus you will change the background matrix of the consensus consciousness.

Stand for yourself and against nothing. Give intent to be all you can be, and commit to taking any action necessary to achieve this. Your *essence* will hear you and bring you to the place of presence in the optimum way and timing for you.

Finally

In many ways *Spiritual Intelligence* can be regarded as natural intelligence. It is not an intellectual quality. It is primarily experiential, taking me ever deeper into the mystery that I am. This is an inherent spirituality, whether it conforms to a recognized discipline or not. It acknowledges the shamanic principle that *Spirit* walks in each one of us, and our highest purpose is to manifest this in our lives for ourselves.

If we are to achieve this we must disregard the highly charged emotional ranting of zealots and fundamentalists. We must let go of any fear of damnation for daring to consider blasphemous ideas. We might even see that the concept of blasphemy in itself is something of a non-sequitur; it resides in the idea that an omnipotent power is incapable of protecting itself from the creatures it presides over.

We might begin to see that what has been referred to variously as collective consciousness, the Holy Spirit, the Source and the great void, is what science is coming to recognize as an intrinsic quality of existence. When the collapse of the concept of observer objectivity is fully in the public domain, we might see that the non-material consciousness that operates through us is the primary essence of all there is.

The extraordinary potential that we all carry is never more needed than now at this time in human history. We each carry generations of baggage within us, passed on by our ancestors, learned from our cultures, inflicted on us by our environment. The weight of these burdens is causing humanity at large to lash out in pain – both self-destructively and towards those we love, as well as towards those we have been taught to see as less than we are. All of the wars and trouble spots in the world, the current wave of terrorism and violence serve to highlight that the unresolved wounds within that we deny are proving to be an unbearable strain as we perpetuate them in the world.

A great master once said: "Ask, and you shall receive." There is a lot of skepticism and disbelief regarding the simplicity of this maxim. Many have spent years praying and felt that their prayers have gone unheard and unanswered. The key to this disillusionment may just be that we have forgotten how to listen, forgotten how to *receive*. What must be re-learned is how to listen to the subtle energies within our bodies, within our feelings, received by our minds and experienced in our lives.

When we invite *Spiritual Intelligence* to show us how to access, how to interpret, and how to act on the organic wisdom that the universe is sharing with us what we already know at a deep unarticulated level inside ourselves is remembered and brought out. This is something that has been known esoterically down the ages, and has been the province of spiritual masters. I invite you to discover that you can align with it through your intent and commitment, and be the master.

Everything I have shared in this book comes under the jurisdiction of universal law, which demonstrates itself through experience – phenomenology and empiricism, rather than hard science and rationalism. Of course it is not conventional ... yet!

Endnotes

a Ambrose Bierce: *The Devil's Dictionary*, Bloomsbury, London 2003 (First published c1911).

b Jacques Lacan: "The agency of the letter in the unconscious ...", in *Écrits: A Selection*, trans. Alan Sheridan (London: Tavistock/Routledge, 1977); original publication *Écrits*, (Paris, Seuil, 1966).

c *A Course In Miracles*, pub. The Foundation for Inner Peace; Tiburon, California, 1975.

d C. G. Jung: "On the Nature of the Psyche", in *The Structure and Dynamics of the Psyche: Collected Works of C. G. Jung*, vol. 8, trans. R. F. C. Hull, (London: Routledge & Kegan Paul, 1960; second edition 1969). Original publication as "Theoretische Überlegungen zum Wesen des Psychischen," *Von den Wurzeln des Bewusstseins* (Zurich: Rascher, 1954).

e Fritjof Capra: *The Tao of Physics*, (London: Wildwood House, 1975; revised, London: Flamingo, 1992).

f Sigmund Freud: "Negation." Trans. Joan Riviere (1925), revised 1950, modified London: Hogarth, 1961. Reprinted in *On Metapsychology: The Theory of Psychoanalysis*. [The Pelican Freud Library, vol. 11. Ed. Angela Richards.] Original publication: Imago, 1925.

g Eckhart Tolle: *The Power of Now*, pub. Hodder & Stoughton, 1999.

The Quest
Joycelin Dawes

What is your sense of soul? Although we may each understand the word differently, we treasure a sense of who we are, what it is to be alive and awareness of an inner experience and connection with "something more." In *The Quest* you explore this sense of soul through a regular practice based on skills of spiritual reflection and be reviewing the story of your life journey, your encounter with spiritual experience and your efforts to live in a sacred way.

Here you become the teller and explorer of your own story. You can find your own answers. You can deepen your spiritual life through the wisdom and insight of the world's religious traditions. You can revisit the building blocks of your beliefs and face the changes in your life. You can look more deeply at wholeness and connection and make your contribution to finding a new and better way.

So well written, constructed and presented, by a small independent group of individuals with many years experience in personal and spiritual growth, education and community, that it is a joy to work with. It is a life-long companion on the spiritual path and an outstanding achievement; it is a labour of love, created with love to bring more love into our world. Susanna Michaelis, *Caduceus*

1 903816 93 9
£9.99/$16.95

Soul Power
Nikki de Carteret

How do you create inner stability in times of chaos? How do you cultivate the power of presence? Where does humility meet mastery? These are just some of the threads of spiritual inquiry that Nikki weaves into a tapestry of Soul Power. Juxtaposing fascinating teachings from the ancient mystics with stories of modern seekers, as well as her own extraordinary journey towards wholeness, she invites you to explore the factors that drain your spiritual energy, and what transformational forces restore it.

I have, quite simply, never before read a book that made me feel so keenly the love of God. Joy Parker, author of *Woman Who Glows in the Dark*.

A beautiful and touching expression of the spiritual journey. Barbara Shipka, author of *Leadership in a Challenging World.*

A unique combination of scholarly research and hands-on experience. Michael Rymer, Hollywood film director

Nikki de Carteret holds a master's degree from the Sorbonne in medieval mystic literature and leads workshops around the world on personal and organizational transformation.

1 903816 17 3
£9.99 $14.95

The 7 Aha!s of Highly Enlightened Souls
Mike George

With thousands of insights now flooding the market place of spiritual development, how do we begin to decide where to start our spiritual journey? What are the right methods? This book strips away the illusions that surround the modern malaise we call stress. In 7 insights, it reminds us of the essence of all the different paths of spiritual wisdom. It succinctly describes what we need to realize in order to create authentic happiness and live with greater contentment. It finishes with the 7 AHA!S, the "eureka moments", the practice of any one of which will profoundly change your life in the most positive way.

Mike George is a spiritual teacher, motivational speaker, retreat leader and management development facilitator. He brings together the three key strands of his millennium-spiritual and emotional intelligence, leadership development, and continuous learning. His previous books include *Discover Inner Peace, Learn to Relax* and *In The Light of Meditation*.

Healing Hands
David Vennells

Hand reflexology is one of the most well-known and respected complementary therapies, practised in many hospitals, surgeries, hospices, health and healing centres, and is enjoying a growing popularity. *Healing Hands* explains the simple techniques of Hand Reflexology so clearly, with the aid of illustrations, that "within a few days the reader could be competently treating themselves or others." It is aimed at those interested in learning the practical techniques (how to give yourself and others a full treatment), and also includes the fascinating history of reflexology, how it works with the hands and the various things we can do to support the healing process. As the reader learns the techniques step by step, they can gradually increase their knowledge of anatomy and physiology, together with developing a more accurate awareness of the hand reflexes and how to treat them accurately and successfully.

David Vennells is a Buddhist teacher of Reiki and the author of *Reiki Mastery* (O Books).

1 903816 81 5
£9.99/$16.95

Humming Your Way to Happiness
An introduction to Tuva and Overtone singing from around the world
Peter Galgut

Ancient peoples have always used incantations and music to tune into nature and achieve expanded consciousness, better health, and for purposes of divination. The most powerful of all forms of sound healing and transformation is the technique of overtone chant, still practiced in many parts of the world today.

This guide shows you how to calm and focus the mind through singing the ancient way. It draws on sources from around the world, covering Pythagorean, Eastern, Jewish, Christian, American and African musical traditions. It covers ancient beliefs in the Lost Chords, Music of the Spheres, Tantras, Chakras, the Kabbalistic tree as well as modern concepts of white sound, brainwave generation and others. It is full of techniques and tips on how to keep "on top", using sound, music and harmony, helping you to take control of your life in your own way in your own time.

Dr Peter Galgut is a medical scientist and clinician at London University, as well as a qualified Acupuncturist and Homeopath.

1 905047 14 2
£9.99 $16.95

O

is a symbol of the world,
of oneness and unity. O Books
explores the many paths of wholeness and spiritual understanding which
different traditions have developed down
the ages. It aims to bring this knowledge in
accessible form, to a general readership, pro-
viding practical spirituality to today's seekers.

For the full list of over 200 titles covering:
ACADEMIC/THEOLOGY • ANGELS • ASTROLOGY/
NUMEROLOGY • BIOGRAPHY/AUTOBIOGRAPHY
• BUDDHISM/ENLIGHTENMENT • BUSINESS/LEADERSHIP/
WISDOM • CELTIC/DRUID/PAGAN • CHANNELLING
• CHRISTIANITY; EARLY • CHRISTIANITY; TRADITIONAL
• CHRISTIANITY; PROGRESSIVE • CHRISTIANITY;
DEVOTIONAL • CHILDREN'S SPIRITUALITY • CHILDREN'S
BIBLE STORIES • CHILDREN'S BOARD/NOVELTY • CREATIVE
SPIRITUALITY • CURRENT AFFAIRS/RELIGIOUS • ECONOMY/
POLITICS/SUSTAINABILITY • ENVIRONMENT/EARTH
• FICTION • GODDESS/FEMININE • HEALTH/FITNESS
• HEALING/REIKI • HINDUISM/ADVAITA/VEDANTA
• HISTORY/ARCHAEOLOGY • HOLISTIC SPIRITUALITY
• INTERFAITH/ECUMENICAL • ISLAM/SUFISM
• JUDAISM/CHRISTIANITY • MEDITATION/PRAYER
• MYSTERY/PARANORMAL • MYSTICISM • MYTHS
• POETRY • RELATIONSHIPS/LOVE • RELIGION/
PHILOSOPHY • SCHOOL TITLES • SCIENCE/
RELIGION • SELF-HELP/PSYCHOLOGY
• SPIRITUAL SEARCH • WORLD
RELIGIONS/SCRIPTURES • YOGA

Please visit our website,
www.O-books.net